London Police Stations

EILEEN SANDERSON

AMBERLEY

To Sandra and Jon

First published 2020

Amberley Publishing
The Hill, Stroud,
Gloucestershire, GL5 4EP

www.amberley-books.com

ISBN 978 1 3981 0016 9 (print)
ISBN 978 1 3981 0017 6 (ebook)

British Library Cataloguing in Publication Data.
A catalogue record for this book is available from the British Library.

Typeset in 10pt on 13pt Celeste.
Typesetting by SJmagic DESIGN SERVICES, India.
Printed in the UK.

Contents

Acknowledgements

The author and publisher would like to thank the following people and organisations for permission to use copyright material in this book: the daughter and granddaughter of George Bramwell Vint, Christine Gibbins and Polly Lines; Peter Kennison, David Swinden and Alan Moss for use of factual material from their three volume research into the history of policing in London. My thanks to the following for their help in the writing of this book: Ron Bishop, Marylyn Coleclough, Chris Dennis, David Hammond, Jonathan Oates at Ealing Archives, Ralph Osborn, Peter Salt, Panayiotis Sinnos, Alison Slade, Clare Smith at the Metropolitan Police Heritage Centre and Connor Stait at Amberley Publishing. Thank you to Kelvin Sanderson for his support and accompanying me on photograph forays.

Every attempt has been made to seek permission for copyright material used in this book. However, if we have inadvertently used copyright material without permission or acknowledgement we apologise, and we will make the necessary correction at the first opportunity.

All photographs are the copyright of the author with the exception of the image on page 12, Cannon Row Police Station from London Metropolitan Archives, City of London COLLAGE: The London Picture Archive reference 176446; the top image on page 21, Tottenham Court Road Police Station, copyright Christine Gibbins; and the image on page 80, Ealing Police Station, copyright Ealing Archives. The image on page 26 is from the author's collection.

Introduction

Londoners are aware that there are huge changes taking place in the policing of London at the present time. Police stations have been quietly closed piecemeal over the last few years, most with little publicity. Some police stations have had improvements, such as large extensions, or the old buildings have been closed down and the station relocated elsewhere in the same area. Examples of this are Ilford Police Station, Wood Green Police Station, Belgravia and Forest Gate Police Station. The current plan is for one central police station, such as the revamped Forest Gate or Charing Cross, to remain open twenty-four hours a day in each London borough.

The Metropolitan Police have also been faced with budgetary restraints, technological change, and the need to be more transparent and accountable, plus the effect of different government policies which have all resulted in a change in the nature of policing.

The Metropolitan Police is now under the command of its first Woman Commissioner in 190 years. Body cameras have been introduced, armed officers are a common sight and vehicles and officers are geared up to carry more equipment than ever before. At the same time there are fewer police officers and more civilian staff carrying out work that had previously been the domain of a trained officer. Police officers are not as visible on the streets and their work is top heavy with administration and monitoring of statistics. Parallel to these changes, the crime rate is rising, and the nature of criminal activity has also changed. Today we seldom hear of the safebreaker, but often hear about the thief on a moped who steals mobile phones, watches and handbags from people. Moreover, the use of CCTV in streets, shops and private properties means that much of the criminal activity can be traced, but this work is labour intensive, needing manpower and time.

This book is a look at the physical presence of police stations on our high streets and in our communities at a time of change. It is mainly a pictorial record of these buildings as they exist now while these changes are occurring. There is also information about each building and sometimes a brief history of an event or incident which has occurred at the station or in the area of the police station.

Many of the police stations that were scheduled to close in 2017 have not done so. Some just stand empty, but others are still used by the Metropolitan Police, though not as the kind of police station that the public has previously known – a place open day and night where arrested people can be held, or the public can obtain advice and report crime or lost and found property. The recent government announcement that there will be extra police recruited to the Metropolitan Police may see a review of the future use of some London police stations.

The aesthetics of the architecture varies. How functional the buildings were meeting the needs of the largest police force in the United Kingdom during the twenty-first century has not been addressed here, but I am sure that many are not up to the standard necessary to carry out policing these days. It is debatable whether they should be removed from local areas where a police presence may benefit the community, reduce the level of crime and reduce the fear of local crime.

CHAPTER 1

Metropolitan Police Stations

The Metropolitan Police was formed in 1829 and the Marine River Police, which had been policing the Thames since 1798, came under the control of the Metropolitan Police in 1837. The Metropolitan Police inherited a number of watch houses as the policing of London had been carried out by a body of men known as 'the watch' who were organised by the parish. It was carried out until the end of the seventeenth century by householders patrolling the streets on a rota basis and questioning or apprehending people suspected of being up to no good. Some of the householders paid others to do the job for them as it could be dangerous, and this really marks the start of paid policing in London. Watchmen were supervised by a constable who was paid to carry out this work.

In the early 1970s my grandmother, talking about policing in Victorian Tottenham, said that her mother remembered my great grandfather and great grandmother talking about 'the Charlies':

> They were the men who acted similar to the police. All along the Criterion Buildings, there was a row of large trees. I don't know if they were oak or not, but near one there was a big wooden tent or box affair in which a man, or men used to keep watch and call out the time during the night. I think the householders used to give so much a week to these men. Sometimes a few rowdies going home late at night would tip the shelter up and make it hard for the men to get free.[1]

The watch house was used for the men to report for duty and to hold criminals until they went to court the following day and was usually built next to the parish church burial ground so they could also protect the burial ground from body-snatchers.[2]

When the Metropolitan Police was set up it had to improve the system for providing police bases and secure accommodation for prisoners. Often buildings were leased and used as police stations in the early years after 1829, and in some areas the old watch houses were retained until more suitable places to be used as police stations could be found.

In 1860 at Church End, Finchley, behaviour of prisoners in the cage, as local schoolchildren walked by, led the vestry to demand that the cage was closed down, but the Metropolitan Police insisted on keeping it until 1880, by which time over 145 people had been detained since 1855.[3]

The first purpose-built police station was in 1831 at Bow Street and new stations were erected throughout the nineteenth century. The buildings were often situated on the high street which made them not only visible and part of the community, but also easily accessible to the public. There was a surge of new police stations from the 1880s which tied in with increased political unrest as well as high profile murders such as those of prostitutes in the East End. [4]

The design of the police station varied depending on different political or social concerns. During the 1880s a new design was introduced providing separate accommodation for police officers and prisoners because there had been a diphtheria case in Rotherhithe Police Station. Following police demonstrations at Bow Street in the 1890s, the decision was then made to accommodate constables in the police station where senior officers could supervise them and prevent any further disobedience among the ranks. By 1895 it was normal practice to provide police accommodation within the new designs for the police stations and there would also be separate secure cell accommodation for prisoners and separate entrances for police, prisoners and the public. [5]

The facilities were poor as it was communal living and there were no areas where a constable who may have been patrolling for hours in the rain could dry his uniform and footwear ready for his next shift.[6]

The Metropolitan Police Force appointed 'The Receiver for the Metropolitan District' who dealt with the financial aspects of the police force and also the funding of new police stations. In 1842 a 'Surveyor of the Police Establishment' was appointed to list all the police buildings and inspect their condition.[7]

The first notable surveyor was Charles Reeves (1815–1866) who started in November 1843. He had 125 properties to deal with when he took over, although a large number of these were old watch houses or rented properties. While holding this post he was responsible for opening twenty-nine new police stations in north and north-east London.

By 1861 his job title had changed, and he was called 'Surveying Inspector of Common Lodging Houses and Surveyor of Dangerous Structures' and he had a Deputy Surveyor and two Assistant Surveyors to help him. Reeves introduced better designed stations, realising that there was a need to provide cells, office space and also accommodation for police officers and he was critical of the conditions some of the police officers had to work in, especially in the old watch houses.

After Charles Reeves died he was succeeded by Thomas Sorbey (1836–1924) who designed police stations at East India Road and Lea Bridge Road, but left the post after a short while before going on to emigrate to Canada to work as an architect.

Sorbey was succeeded by Frederick H. Caiger (fl. 1865–1873) who had been the Deputy Surveyor and had been working as Assistant Surveyor since 1850. Caiger's deputy was John Butler who had been working as a 'Clerk of Works' when Reeves had been in charge. In 1881 John Butler became Surveyor, by which period they had opened another ten police stations. This was increased to twenty-one stations by 1895.

John Butler was succeeded by his son, John Dixon Butler (1861–1920), who held the position of Surveyor from 1895 until his death in 1920 and designed over 200 police stations and courts. He worked with Norman Shaw on the extensions to New Scotland Yard and was made a Fellow of the Royal Institute of British Architects.

CHAPTER 2

Central London Police Stations

Bow Street Police Station

Bow Street Police Station was an iconic police station which sadly closed down in 1992 when it was amalgamated with Cannon Row, forming the new Charing Cross Police Station. Charing Cross Police Station is on the site of the old Charing Cross Hospital which was designed by Decimus Burton (1800–1881), whose other designs included the Palm House at Kew Gardens and some of the London Zoo buildings. The station is undergoing refurbishment and modernisation at a cost of £35 million.

The police lamps introduced outside police stations from 1861 were traditionally blue in colour, but Bow Street Police Station had white ones because when Queen Victoria visited the Royal Opera House, which is situated opposite Bow Street Police Station and Court, she was reminded of the blue room where her husband, Prince Albert, had died. In 1972 a letter to a newspaper said:

> Why must the fine gothic lanterns outside Bow Street Police Station now show a blue lamp? Queen Victoria spared us this sight on leaving the Royal Opera House, and now gone is another story from the past. I think it very sad.[1]

Bow Street is the site of the first police office and the first London magistrates' court.[2] It is associated with the Bow Street Runners, the early London police force set up in 1748/9 to investigate and detect offenders. In 1729 Sir Thomas De Veil, who was known as the first honest magistrate, set up in Bow Street in 1729 and his 'office' was seen as the best way to street-level justice in London.[3] A Mounted Patrol was established in Bow Street by De Veil's successors, John and Henry Fielding, but the patrols were short lived due to lack of funding. In 1805 new uniformed Horse Patrols were introduced followed by a night-time Foot Patrol the following year.

The Metropolitan Police had taken over an ancient watch house in St Paul's Churchyard which was found to be inadequate for police use, so relocated these headquarters of Covent Garden police division to 'Station House' at 33–34 Bow Street.[4]

The Bow Street Runners were amalgamated with the Metropolitan Police in 1829 and the 1839 Metropolitan Police Act started to define Magistrates as stipendiary, rather than independent which paved the way for the Home Office to take over 3 and 4 Bow Street in 1842 where the magistrates were based.[5] By 1860 this building was no longer suitable for use by the Metropolitan Police as it needed a great deal of work done on it, so a ninety-nine-year lease was taken out on another site in 1876. The site was across the road from Nos 3 and 4 and it was adjacent to the police station at 33–34 Bow Street.

Sir John Taylor from the Office of Works designed the new building and it was opened in 1881, consisting of a purpose-built police station, a magistrates' court and a section house for 106 police officers.

Bow Street Police Station and Magistrates' Court are Grade II listed buildings made of Portland Stone and they are described as 'dignified eclectic Graeco-Roman with some Vanbrughian details'.[6]

It remained an important police station, partly because of the link to the early formation of the police through the Bow Street Runners, and partly because of its vicinity to the West End and its close relationship with the Magistrates' Court in the same building. Many famous people have appeared in the court, often being charged for the offence at Bow Street Police Station and held in their cells.

A journalist reporting on the last day at Bow Street Court before it closed down lists Charles Dickens, Casanova and the Kray Brothers as people who had appeared in the court.[7] He commented on the gangland killers, the suspected terrorists and the wayward politicians, but also acknowledged the 'bread and butter' of the courts – the petty criminals, busy falling foul of the law in the middle of London. It would have been an incredibly busy court which would have been chaotically busy, noisy and often unpleasant. The chief magistrate, Tim Workman, said that,

> The present dock – a mere 125 years old – has among its occupants Oscar Wilde, Dr Crippen and the Kray twins and more recently, cases involving General Pinochet and cases of persons suspected of terrorist offences both here and abroad have been heard in this court.[8]

Bow Street Police Station, Bow Street, London, WC2 (1881–1992).

On 17 April 1984 Yvonne Fletcher, an unarmed police officer based at Bow Street Police Station, was on duty at an anti-Gaddafi demonstration at St James's Square where she was fatally shot in the back by a person or persons inside the Libyan Embassy and another eleven people were injured.[9] No one has yet been charged with this murder. It led the film producer Michael Winner to write:

> It would serve to indicate that not everyone in this country takes seeming pleasure in attacking the police in the execution of their difficult duties, but that most of us regard their conduct and bravery, under a whole series of endless and varied provocations, as demonstrably noble and worthy of our thanks.[10]

There were so many donations after her death that it led to the formation of the Police Memorial Trust whose aims are to erect memorials to police officers killed in the line of duty.

There is a memorial to Yvonne Fletcher at St James's Square and a cherry tree was also planted in her memory in 1984 in the Square. Sadly the memorial was defaced in January 2019, but has now been replaced. Considering the number of police memorials which have since been laid to those who have been killed in London, they seem to have had relatively little vandalism.

A further letter published from Winner said that he could

> See a day in the future when human memory, being what it is, has discarded the events that now seem so important, and the shadows from the trees above sway slowly to and fro on the pavement of St James's Square, the sunlight catching a small Memorial.[11]
>
> Maybe two people passing by will stop and one will say to the other – 'Yvonne Fletcher? Who was she'? There is a simple and noble answer: she was a member of the British Police Force.[12]

In 1961 an 'Identikit' was used for the first time by the Police at Bow Street Police Station to build up a physical picture of the murderer of Elsie Batten at Cecil Court.[13]

The police station closed in 1992 and the Magistrates' Court in 2006, with the building being converted into a hotel which will also include a Bow Street police museum.

Cannon Row Police Station

The station was built between 1898 and 1902 by John Dixon Butler with R. Norman Shaw as consultant as part of the New Scotland Yard extension. It is an amalgam of Flemish and English Baroque sources continuing Shaw's original New Scotland Yard theme.[14] It was situated very close to New Scotland Yard which had the knock-on effect of bringing fame to the station because notable Scotland Yard detective squads would often take high-profile prisoners there for questioning.[15]

An unscheduled stop in Britain by the ship carrying the spy, Mata Hari, led to her arrest and subsequent detention at Cannon Row Police Station in 1916. She was questioned by Assistant Commissioner Sir Basil Thomson and the interview can be heard at The National

Cannon Row Police Station, Cannon Row, Westminster, SW1 (1902–1985). (Copyright: Cannon Row Police Station from London Metropolitan Archives, City of London COLLAGE: The London Picture Archive reference 176446)

Archives, along with a Metropolitan Police-written list of items found on her at the time of arrest.[16] She was executed in France in 1917.

The station was relocated to the nearby Curtis Green Building then transferred to Charing Cross Police Station in 1992. The old Victorian building is now part of the Scotland Yard complex.

Gerald Road Police Station

A building was first leased for use by the Metropolitan Police at Gerald Road, which was then known as Cottage Row in 1845, and called the rather quaint sounding 'Cottage Road Police Station'. A Surveyors' report of 1881 into the conditions of Metropolitan police stations stated that the station was 'a very cramped site'.[17] It was renamed Gerald Road in 1885 and the freehold was obtained in 1891.[18]

It was reconstructed in 1925 but closed down in 1993 when Belgravia Police Station was opened, and is now a private residence. Belgravia Police Station has also closed its front office as policing of the area will be covered by the refurbished Charing Cross Police Station.

Gerald Road Police
Station, Gerald Road,
Pimlico, London, SW1
(1885–1993).

Gerald Road Police Station is still remembered locally by some long-term residents due to local press coverage for the awards it used to win for its flower displays. There is film footage from 1957 of officers watering the flowers and the narrative ends by saying that Gerald Road 'has a proud anti-crime record but then of course the place is so attractive it must almost be a pleasure to be detained there.'[19] When it was operational Ronnie Biggs apparently spent a night here.

The routine arrest of two drunken men who were taken to Gerald Road Police Station started events which led to the formation of 'The Metropolitan Police Union' in 1913, and the introduction of the Police Federation Staff Association. One of the men arrested was a Mr Costa, who had actually been trying to get into his own home while drunk and disorderly. Neither his wife nor his neighbours wanted to press charges.[20] However, the arrested men still had to be entered in a 'Refused Charge Book'. Inspector John Syme had refused to charge the men and defended the arresting constables when they were reprimanded and disciplined over the matter and Syme was transferred.[21] He was assessed as being unreasonable and too familiar with his subordinates; he protested to the Commissioner but was then suspended while his complaint was investigated. Following the investigation, he was demoted, but decided he would contact his MP and was then dismissed from the Metropolitan Police.[22] The editor of the *Police Review* took up his case but Syme's behaviour became more erratic and he was prosecuted and jailed for threats to the Home Secretary and a superior officer.

After his release he formed the John Syme League and the following year the League announced in the *Police Review* that the Metropolitan Police Union had been formed. The editor of the *Police Review* had been supportive and campaigned for improvements in pay and conditions but did not want to be supporting a police union which had the right to strike.[23] He urged his readers to consider a Police Federation which would protect the rights of its members but not strike. Syme was again arrested and charged in 1914 with publishing a defamatory libel publication *Fighting Officialdom; A Home Office Persecution* about the Metropolitan Police Commissioner, Sir Edward Henry.[24] He served another

13

prison sentence but became unstable, serving further prison sentences for threatening to kill the Prince of Wales and libel.[25]

In 1924 a Lord Chancellor's Committee was set up to inquire into the affair and concluded that Syme's dismissal had been justified, but his initial behaviour had been correct and that the disciplinary action had been heavy-handed.[26] Seven years later his integrity was acknowledged, and it was agreed he had been wrongly transferred and his pension was paid back-dated to 1909 – over £1,200, but by this time Syme was mentally fragile.[27]

In 1922 two London-based members of the IRA assassinated Field Marshal Sir Henry Wilson and the ensuing chase by police and members of the public passed by Gerald Road Police Station. Two off-duty officers who were in the section house above the station heard the noise and jumped from a first-floor window and chased the two men. Shots were fired by the two suspects and when one of them tried to reload his revolver one police officer hit him on the head with his truncheon dazing him sufficiently to make an arrest.[28]

Hyde Park Police Station

Although Hyde Park Police Station is still operational, it has been included in this book as it is a listed Metropolitan Police building situated in the protected site of a major park.

Secondary constables from the Metropolitan Police assisted the park staff in policing the park until 1867 when the Metropolitan Police took over policing the park.[29] The Royal Parks were policed by the Royal Parks Police and only Hyde Park was policed by the Metropolitan Police.[30]

The Household Cavalry barracks in the park were taken over by the police in 1867 and a new police station was built in 1902 which incorporated stables and a section house.[31] In 1972 the section house was closed, but the accommodation was used as a 'feeding station' for large groups of officers when they were deployed on demonstrations and large events in central London.[32] A Royal Parks Operational Unit was set up by the Metropolitan Police in 2004 and they took over responsibility for policing the Royal Parks.

Hyde Park Police Station, Hyde Park, London, W1 (1902–present day).

Marble Arch Police Station
at Marble Arch, London W1
(police station 1851–1950).

Marble Arch Police Station

Surprisingly there was a small police station at the top of Marble Arch looking down over Park Lane. It was situated on 'D' Division (Marylebone) and Marylebone police officers were issued a key with their uniform to access the station until at least the 1970s. It only consists of a few small rooms which were cold, sparse and dismal. However, in spite of its size the Metropolitan Police requested permission to use the rooms in 1851 for accommodation for six single men and 'in times of public commotion it would admit a considerable body of Police being assembled at this important point'.[33]

A police officer interviewed for an oral history on his time at Marylebone Lane during the 1950s reflected on the task of directing traffic around Marble Arch and he described it as a 'nightmare', with traffic coming at the officer from all directions! He says that this task was often given to new probationers or as he called them 'the youngsters'.[34]

The 'nightmare' became even worse when the officer on number one beat at Marble Arch was appointed to ensure the safe transport of the Royal Horse Artillery from their barracks in St John's Wood, along with their heavy gun carriages, through the Arch and into Hyde Park. This happened on a very regular basis.

Marylebone Police Station

By 1864 Marylebone Lane Police Station had been designated to 'D' division and remained part of this division throughout its history in spite of many other police stations being moved into different divisional areas when various reorganisations of the Metropolitan boundaries occurred.[35] The area 'D' division covered did alter over the years but included the area north of Oxford Street, west of Portland Place and east of Edgware Road. By the 1970s this area had extended to Tottenham Court Road as well.

The Earl of Oxford erected a building to be used as a watch house and lock-up in Marylebone. It would have been situated near the rear of the present-day Debenhams in

Oxford Street.[36] It was designed by James Gibbs and had a coat of arms over the door which was engraved by Michael Rysbrack with the retrospective date of 1729.[37] In 1803 the plans to enlarge and replace the watch house went ahead and it opened in 1804. The fireplace had the words 'Be Sober – Be Vigilant' engraved above it.[38]

A new courthouse was built in 1824/5 and the old courthouse at the south end of the watch house building fell into disuse. A 1901 account states that there were cells at the old courthouse which were in an odd arrangement accessed through the front door. More strangely the cell grill did not have bars, but interwoven strips which were commonly used in the sixteenth century.[39] It has been suggested that the old courthouse had included a much earlier parish lock-up.[40] In 1829 the Metropolitan Police took over the watch house and it was returned to the vestry in about 1858.[41]

The old watch house was sold to Debenhams and was extended to accommodate an old bookshop which had belonged to an Edward Bumpus and was renamed the 'Old Watch House' in 1921.[42] The watch house kept its cells and the shop became very popular, with authors such as George Bernard Shaw, T. E. Lawrence and J. M. Barrie making appearances there.[43] A *Lewis Carroll Exhibition* was held at the old court house in 1932, but by 1935 the road had been widened and the buildings were demolished and replaced by a neo-Georgian block which was later made into a hotel and restaurant.[44]

In 1859 a new police station opened at 69 Welbeck Street.[45] The front of the building was designed to look like a private residence, along with a separate entrance 'for the superior officers only'.[46]

In 1881 it was described in the Metropolitan Police Surveyor's report into conditions in Metropolitan Police Stations as 'two blocks – one an old dwelling-house in Welbeck Street, used as offices and partly for bedrooms, and a purposely built small station, with charge room, cells etc. The mess arrangements are very bad. We found a constable shaving and dressing in the back area'.[47]

By 1892 the freehold for the houses at 48 and 50 Marylebone Lane, backing onto Welbeck Street, had been bought and became operational.[48] The building was designed by John Dixon Butler who again re-designed it twenty years later.

By the early 1930s there were problems with the building as there was no yard and the 'roadway outside the station was so narrow that a car – much less cars – cannot remain for long without causing real obstruction'.[49] By this time the area had changed from being mainly residential and was a busy retail and commercial area and it was decided to relocate the police station to near Madam Tussauds in the Baker Street area. The war disrupted these plans and by the 1950s the new plan was to use a site in Seymour Street, which is at the back of Oxford Street and at the top end of Wigmore Street and runs parallel to Oxford Street.[50]

During the building of the station two four-storey Georgian houses had to be demolished and it ended up with the evacuation of fifty people as it looked as if the adjacent buildings were about to collapse.[51] Photographs in the Metropolitan Police Heritage Centre show the interiors of the Georgian houses with beautiful internal decoration and lovely leaded glass windows.

The new station was opened in 1977 but was closed down in 2012 and the Portman Estate lease was sold for £3 million. The site is 78,500 square feet and extends from Old Quebec Street, where the old Robert Mark Section House stood, over to Seymour Street which faced onto Portman Square and is in a prime location as it is so near Oxford Street. It is now residential and office accommodation with space for restaurants.

Marylebone Police Station, Seymour Street, London, W1 (1977–2013).

In 1963 the station charged Dr Stephen Ward with his involvement in the Profumo affair and he was held overnight in the cells.[52]

A newspaper article from 1897 said that,

The officers and men of the D Division of Police yesterday presented a gold watch to Miss Florence Smith, at Marylebone Police Station, in appreciation of her conduct in assisting a constable who was ejecting a man from the Marylebone Music Hall. Miss Smith, seeing that no one went to the constable's assistance pushed her way through the crowd, and blew his whistle with the result that other constables were quickly summoned.[53]

Molyneux Street Police Station (also known as Crawford Place or John Street Police Station)

Following the purchase of several freehold properties and the Horse and Groom public house, a police station was set up in 1849 in Molyneux Street, which is situated near the Edgware Road and quite near Paddington.

The Surveyor's report into the condition of Metropolitan Police Stations in 1881 stated that it was:

Two adjoining blocks erected at different periods. Cells have been added in the yard. The station is important. The space very confined. The rooms are badly shaped for large dormitories. The water closets are underground and unsatisfactory. More cells are required.[54]

The same site was used for a police section house, which was built *c.* 1930s, called Elliot Section House. It has recently been demolished and made into private residential apartments.

The site backs onto Cato Street, which is now a small Mews type road, but in 1820 one of the houses was the location of the 'Cato Street Conspiracy' whereby radicals plotted to murder the Cabinet as they dined at Grosvenor Square by beheading them. The plot was uncovered, and Cato Street was stormed, and one policeman was killed.[55]

Site of Molyneux Police Station and later Elliot House, Police Section House. The site was used by the Metropolitan Police from *c.* 1849–2006.

New Scotland Yard and Scotland Yard

'Scotland Yard' is a name synonymous with the Metropolitan Police. The police headquarters were based at 4 Whitehall Place (apart from 999 the number most associated with the Metropolitan Police is Whitehall 1212) and access to headquarters was through a court called Great Scotland Yard, which backed onto 4 Whitehall Place and the term 'Scotland Yard' began to be used colloquially to refer to the Metropolitan Police Headquarters.[56]

By 1887 a number of buildings in Whitehall Place and Great Scotland Yard were used by the police and they included a police station, stables, offices and accommodation for the Commissioner. In 1890 the headquarters were moved to Victoria Embankment SW1, adjacent to Cannon Row Police Station and into a Gothic-style purpose-built building designed by Norman Shaw (1831–1912) and called New Scotland Yard. After the Second World War additions were made to the building by Curtis Green.[57]

The Great Scotland Yard complex was rebuilt in 1910 and used by the Ministry of Defence with soldiers enlisting at the building for both the First World War and the Second

Old Scotland Yard, Great Scotland Yard, London, SW1 2015 (*c.* 1910).

World War. It has retained an early nineteenth-century house at the rear, but the main building in Great Scotland Yard is now a police-themed luxury hotel. The stable area is still a separate building, possibly with the freehold still held by the Metropolitan Police.

In 1967 there was another move of Scotland Yard, this time it was to the junction of the Broadway and Victoria Street. In contrast to the iconic Gothic building by Shaw, the new building was a modernist tower block and the most distinguishable feature was the revolving sign outside which performed over 14,000 revolutions every day.[58]

2016 saw the return of headquarters back to the Victorian Embankment and into a redesigned Curtis Green building. The move also included transferring both the Black Museum and the rotating sign from outside the 1960s building.

Paddington Green Police Station

This station opened in 1971 and closed in 2018. It was prominently situated at the end of the A40 flyover and was the largest and most expensive station built by the Metropolitan Police, costing nearly £1.5 million and becoming the most modern police station in the world at the time.

It had sixteen high-security cells, which were used for high-security prisoners, and was the most secure police station in the United Kingdom. The station and section house are now closed, and the building remains empty.

Above and right: Paddington Green Police Station, Harrow Road, Westminster, W2 (1971–*c.* 2019).

Rochester Row
Police Station,
Rochester Row,
London, SW1
(1901–1993).

Rochester Row Police Station

Rochester Row's first police station was occupied in 1846 and in 1869 married quarters and stables were added as horse transport was the main way of getting around.[59] In 1887 rebuilding took place and included a new section house and a courthouse, with the police station opening in 1901 and Westminster Police Court opening in 1903.[60] These were both designed by John Dixon Butler in a Baroque style, with a large 'oeil de boeuf' window in a triangular pedimented gable.[61]

In the Thames Flood disaster of 1928, the police officers attached to Rochester Row played a major role in providing operational assistance and a charcoal drawing was presented to these officers by the Mayor of Westminster in recognition of their bravery. The drawing was displayed in the station office until the early 1970s.[62] In 1940 the adjacent court was partially destroyed by enemy action.[63]

Tottenham Court Road Police Station

In 1843 a fifty-year lease was taken out on Clarks' Buildings and replaced the old George Street watch house, but a building at 58 Tottenham Court Road was purchased and a new police station opened in 1876, with 19 Whitfield Street and adjoining buildings purchased over the years.[64]

Stronger foundations were laid at the site at 58 Tottenham Court Road as there had probably been a pond as the ground was very muddy.[65] More land was bought, and the station was rebuilt and opened in 1900, closing temporarily during the Second World War. Policing was carried out from nearby 16 and 17 Rathbone Street which had been section houses. The police station was damaged by a lightning strike in August 1935.

Tottenham Court Road Police Station was hit during the Second World War leaving one fatality and five serious injuries.[66] The building was again rebuilt and 'the design of the building reflecting war-time perils had the appearance of a stone fortress'.[67] The building has been demolished and is now a busy Marks & Spencers food store, but there does appear to be remaining parts of the rear of the building still in use by police or British Transport Police.

The architectural drawing in this book of Tottenham Court Road Police Station is by the architect George Bramwell Vint (1913–1983). His daughter recalls that he worked on Whetstone Police Station, the new Paddington Green Police Station, courts and police housing.[68] Both Tottenham Court Road Police Station and Whetstone Police Stations are now closed.

Right: Tottenham Court Road Police Station, 58 Tottenham Court Road, W1 (1942–*c.* 1998). Drawing by George Bramwell Vint (1913–1983). (Copyright Christine Gibbins)

Below: Site of Tottenham Court Road Police Station, 58 Tottenham Court Road, W1 (1942–*c.* 1998). It is now a Marks & Spencer store.

The old Vine Street Police Station Police Lamp which hangs outside Holborn Police Station, Theobalds Road, London, WC1.

Vine Street Police Station

On Tuesday 29 September 1829 the very first Metropolitan Police patrols went on their beats, leaving from Scotland Yard and five of the old watch houses, one of which was Vine Street.[69] The police station at 10 Vine Street was previously the watch house for the parish of St James, but by 1868 the building was demolished and rebuilt and in 1931 it was extended to include the former 'Man in the Moon' public house, which was refurbished and incorporated into the new police building.[70] The 1881 Metropolitan Police Surveyor's report into the conditions of police stations described it as 'a very important station'.[71]

After nearby West End Central Police Station was opened in 1940 Vine Street ceased to function as an operational police station, but was used for various other administrative purposes and from time to time different squads were also based there.[72] However, in 1971 it came into use again as a police station to ease the pressure on nearby busy West End Central Police Station but was finally closed in 1997. The site is now a modern office block and only the name of the adjacent alley gives a brief glimpse of the previous history of the area as the alley is called 'Man in the Moon Alley'.

The Marquess of Queensberry was charged with criminal libel against Oscar Wilde in 1895 at Vine Street Police Station.

Wellington Arch Police Station

Wellington Arch is situated at Hyde Park Corner and was built in 1828. It was designed by Decimus Burton (1800–1881) and is also known as the Constitution Arch or Triumphal Arch. An application was made by the Commissioner of Police to the Secretary of State in 1847 for empty rooms at the top of the Arch to be occupied by police officers as it was

Wellington Arch Police Station at Wellington Arch, Hyde Park Corner, London, SW1 (police station 1831–1992).

a 'great and important thoroughfare'.[73] The 1881 Metropolitan Police Surveyor's report described it as 'an exceptional station. One half of the structure supporting the figure of the Duke of Wellington is used as police lodgings, but the conditions are unsatisfactory, the lighting is bad and there is little or no ventilation'.[74] Wellington was later replaced by Peace descending on the Chariot of War.

It was used as an observation point for traffic and described as a section house as it had accommodation for officers and a kitchen and boot cleaning room but fell into disuse by the police in 1992.[75]

West End Central Police Station

West End Central Police Station, situated in Savile Row near Regent Street, was built to take over the duties of both Vine Street and Great Marlborough Street Police Station, opening on 14 July 1940, but several months later the building was badly damaged by a bomb and more or less gutted. A CID officer was described searching for an exhibit needed for court in the debris while building demolition workers were looking at Criminal Record Office files which had been scattered around the area.[76]

23

The station was designed by Sir John Burnet, Tait & Lorne and displayed at the back modernistic details of Dutch derivation.[77] West End Central has not been credited with architectural attractiveness as it has been described as a 'cruel, stone-faced building – gloomy and unwelcoming – with all the charm of a Victorian workhouse'.[78]

The same source refers to the 'Alumni' as the Richardson gang, the Krays and Christine Keeler 's one-time lover, Lucky Gordon'.[79]

It was a very busy station and dealt with problems associated with prostitution, street crime, pornography and unlicensed gambling. There were problems with police corruption within the division but a strong and largely successful movement to clean up the corruption of officers took place in the 1970s and 1980s. The station became so overcrowded that nearby Vine Street station was reopened in 1971. West End Central Police Station was closed to the public at the end of 2019.

West End Central Police Station, Saville Row, London, W1 (1940–2019).

CHAPTER 3

North London Police Stations

Albany Street Police Station

There was a police station in Albany Street as far back as 1832, but an internal report of 1864 stated that 'the present station at Albany Street was unsuitable for today's requirements'.[1] 'In a sudden emergency the Duty Officer has to send to Somers Town and Portland Town stations for extra men'.[2] The report stated that it had previously been used as the watch house of the Crown Estate, but the present site was good and there was room to build a new station along with accommodation for thirty single men.[3]

The new police station was opened in 1866 and included a section house but was rebuilt again in 1900 and then replaced by another new building in Albany Street in 1960, which was on a different location in Albany Street.[4] Metropolitan Police stations which opened in the 1960s and 1970s, such as Albany Street, Brentford, Marylebone and Paddington Green, embraced the Brutalist style of architecture associated with this period. Albany Street Police Station front office has been closed since 2013.

Albany Street
Police Station,
60 Albany
Street,
Camden, NW1
(1960–2013).

Barnet Police Station, High Street, Barnet, EN5 (*c.* 1907). (author's collection)

Barnet Police Station

Freehold land was purchased from the Manor of Chipping Barnet and East Barnet in 1899 to build a new police station, but the site was deemed to be too small, so the adjoining properties at 28, 30 and 32 Barnet High Street were purchased from the Leather-sellers Company for £1,800 and the new police station was opened in 1916.[5] It was replaced by a completely new building in 1976. The front office is closed to the public and a yellow phone sits outside if a member of the public needs to contact police.

Caledonian Road Police Station

The Home Office authorised the purchase of a piece of land, which was near the new Metropolitan Cattle Market, from a Mr Pocock on a ninety-nine-year lease in 1855. This was for a new police station.[6] A later public house next to the police station was called the Pocock Public House and this pub has now been converted to offices. The movement of cattle from all over the United Kingdom to the cattle market meant that the area was very busy and would have put a strain on the police, especially as the public houses were allowed to stay open during market hours, which meant locals used the pubs as well as the market workers.[7] The Victorian building was rebuilt and reopened in 1917, but was closed down in 1992, having policed the area for nearly 150 years.[8] The building has been converted into residential accommodation.

26

Caledonian Road Police Station, 460 Caledonian Road, Islington, N7 (1917–1992).

Ronald Marwood was an Islington scaffolder who was convicted for the murder of PC Raymond Henry Summers at a dance hall in 1958 and hanged on 8 May 1959. He had been drinking heavily on the night of the murder and then went on the run but handed himself into Caledonian Road Police Station and (under caution) admitted to the murder of PC Summers. When it went to court, he claimed that the constable had punched him and Marwood hit back, but he did not have a weapon on him. Marwood said that the police statement was made up by the police and he had only signed it as he had been at the station too long. After his conviction a street demonstration of about 1,000 people, plus prisoners from within Pentonville, opposed the death penalty for Marwood. Following his execution, Cannon Collins gave a sermon in St Paul's Cathedral stating that the Homicide Act of 1957 should be amended and a few days later a motion was introduced in the House of Commons to abolish capital punishment.[9]

Edmonton Police Station

Edmonton Parish Authorities surrendered a watch house which was next to the railway station to the Metropolitan Police in 1840. It was retained by the police until 1867.[10] In 1865 the freehold for a new site was purchased at 320 Fore Street, with the new station including stables and a section house for single officers, but it was replaced by a new station in 1916, designed by John Dixon Butler and built at the same site in Fore Street. It is a Grade II listed building, designed in an Arts and Crafts style in red brick and Portland stone dressing and bands with a green slated roof.[11]

Edmonton Police Station, 320 Fore Street, Edmonton, N18 (1916–1989).

In the late 1970s computerisation meant that the station had problems with space and overcrowding, so a portacabin was used until the Great Storm of 1987 caused substantial damage to it, but another four portacabins were still added to the site up until 1989, when a new station was opened in the same road. It was officially opened by the Princess of Wales in June 1990 and is still an operational police station manned twenty-four hours a day.[12]

Hampstead Police Station

A number of early magistrates had lived in Cannon Hall in Hampstead from about 1739 and a lock-up, which still exists, was built into the walls of the Hall and was used to detain prisoners until they were dealt with by the magistrates.[13] The lock-up became a garden shed after the Metropolitan Police built the new Hampstead police station in the 1830s.

The new station was in Holly Walk but is a private residence now as land was bought in Rosslyn Hill in 1909 and a new police station and adjoining court, designed by John Dixon Butler, was built and was opened in 1913.[14] It is now a Grade II listed building and the protection includes the stable and harness room, railings and lamps. It is an example of a combined police station and courthouse.[15] A description of the station was a 'Cosy cottage-style station' which was popular with officers and the adjacent public house, 'The Rosslyn Arms', which was nicknamed 'The Annexe'.[16]

The front counter was closed in 2013 and the building had been taken over by squatters by April 2014 but was sold the same year for just over £14 million. There have been planning proposals to turn it into a school.

The last woman to be hanged in Britain was Ruth Ellis who was charged with the murder of her lover in 1955 at Hampstead Police Station.[17]

Hampstead Police Station, Rosslyn Way, Hampstead, NW3 (1913–2013).

Highbury Vale Police Station

In 1902 negotiations with the London County Council for purchasing land in Blackstock Road, which was owned by the Council, for the building of a new police station began. This was followed by legal battles for the compulsory purchase of properties and subsequently Highbury Police Station did not open until 1910. The police station was closed down in 2012 and it has been refurbished and divided into 'boutique apartments' which were for sale for £700,000 each.

Highbury Vale Police Station, 211 Blackstock Road, Islington, N4 (1910–2012).

Highbury Vale Police Station, 211 Blackstock Road, Islington, N4 (1910–2012).

Highgate Police Station

In 1849 a new police station was built in Highgate and the following year the old watch house was surrendered back to the Parish Authorities.[18] The police station was closed down in 1902 and is now a shop. It is a Grade II listed building consisting of yellow stock brick.[19]

It was replaced by a police station in the Archway Road, which was modernised in 1936, but was hit by a V1 Flying Bomb in 1944.[20] It was rebuilt and reopened on the same site in 1960, but has been closed down, completely demolished and the site is now a block of residential flats.

Old Highgate Police Station, Highgate West Hill, N6 (c. 1849–1902).

30

Holborn Police Station and Grays Inn Road Police Station

A purpose-built police station was opened at Grays Inn Road in 1898. It was a three-storey building and was able to house not only the station, but also accommodation for 100 police officers. Police accommodation was only for men as women were not recruited until 1919 and were only provided with a one-year contract with no powers of arrest. It was closed down in 1965 when the new Holborn Police Station was opened in nearby Theobalds Road, but reopened temporarily between 1999 and 2002 when Holborn Police Station was refurbished. Grays Inn Road Police Station has been sold and has been converted into offices.

The new 1960s Holborn Police Station was 155 feet tall and had a 75 feet wireless mast at the top of it, but the original lamp from Vine Street Police Station hangs outside the station.[21]

Ernest Saunders, who was known as one of the 'Guinness Four', was charged at Holborn Police Station with attempting to pervert the course of justice and falsifying documents for his involvement in trying to manipulate the share prices in the Guinness Company. He was convicted in 1990. Holborn police station is scheduled to close.

Holborn Police Station, Theobalds Road, London, WC1 (1965–*c*. 2019)

Grays Inn Road Police Station, Grays Inn Road, Holborn, London, WC1 (1898–1965 and 1999–2002).

Holloway Police Station

Holloway Police station has often been confused with Hornsey Police Station as it lies on the Hornsey Road. An initial building of 1835 was replaced by a new station which opened in 1875.[22] This was refurbished in 1911 but demolished after a bomb hit the building in 1941. Seven police officers were killed, and others were injured in the explosion. A new police station was opened in 1965, with the front counter closing in 2017, although it has still not been sold.

Holloway Police Station, 256 Hornsey Road, Islington, N7 (1965–c. 2017).

Hornsey
Police Station,
98 Tottenham
Lane,
Hornsey, N8
(1915–2017).

Hornsey Police Station

An early lock-up building in Priory Road, Hornsey, was kept as a police station until 1868 when it was returned to the parish and used as a mortuary.[23]

By 1865 Hornsey became part of 'Y' Division. The area in 'Y' Division was large and included Tottenham, Southgate, Enfield, Hornsey, Walthamstow and Chingford.[24] The whole area would be policed mainly by foot and by a limited number of horse patrols by the senior officers.

In 1912 freehold land in Tottenham Lane was bought from Reverend Spinks for a new purpose-built police station which was opened in 1916 and rebuilt in 1936.[25] In 1964 the freehold for the nearby old fire station was purchased and the police station was eventually extended after the old library, which was sandwiched between the police station and the old fire station, was purchased. The front office at Hornsey closed in 2017 and the building has not yet been sold.

Islington Police Station

The Metropolitan Police took over the old watch house and later on took a lease on premises in Birds' Buildings in 1853, followed four years later by the purchase of a freehold site which was bought in Upper Street, Islington.[26] It was rebuilt in 1902 and enlarged in 1913, but closed down in 1992 as it was replaced by a new building in Tolpuddle Street.[27]

The 1902 building at 227 Upper Street still exists and has been converted into private residential accommodation. The Tolpuddle Street Police Station remains a twenty-four hour operational police station and has a modern police lamp outside, along with the earlier blue lamp from the old station in Upper Street.

Above left: Islington Police Station, 277 Upper Street, Islington, N1 (1858–1992).

Above right: Police lamp outside Islington Police Station, 2 Tolpuddle Street, Islington N1 (1992–present day).

Kentish Town Police Station

Kentish Town Police Station was designed by Norman Shaw (1894–1896) and opened in 1896. It was restored in 1984 and is a Grade II listed building constructed in yellow stock brick with three storeys and a round-arched entrance engraved 'Police' with hood mould, fanlight and double panelled doors. The rainwater heads and pipes are original and there are attached cast-iron railings with overthrow having a blue lamp with the word 'Police' on it.[28] The police station still has a front counter open twenty-four hours a day.

Kentish Town Police Station, 12 Holmes Road, Camden Town, NW5 (1896–present day).

Kilburn Police Station, Salusbury Road, Queen's Park, London, NW6 (1980–c. 2019).

Kilburn Police Station

Some houses were converted for use as a police station in 1872, followed by the purchase of land from the Ecclesiastical Commission for a new police station to be built in Kilburn, at Salusbury Road junction with Mortimer Road, which opened in 1889.[29]

In 1938 the police station was closed, and Kilburn policing operated from Harrow Road. The old police station was converted into a section house and then became a Group Reserve Centre at the start of the Second World War.[30] It was hit by three high explosive bombs in 1940 and completely demolished, with fourteen of the eighteen people on duty losing their lives.[31]

Kilburn continued to be policed by Harrow Road Police Station until 1965 when the divisional boundaries were changed. New land was purchased in 1967 and the following year the fire station and the mortuary adjacent to the Kilburn site were bought, with the new station opening in 1980. The opening ceremony was attended by the Home Secretary, William Whitelaw, and one of the guests at the ceremony was retired Station Sergeant William Watson, who had been on duty when the bomb fell on Kilburn in 1940.[32] The front office of the police station is now closed.

Kings Cross Station Police Station

A watch house was set up near St Mary's Church in Upper Street in 1797 to police Kings Cross and a later Kings Cross Police Station was situated beneath a column erected to King George IV, which would have been situated at the Euston Road junction with York Way. This was demolished in 1945.[33]

There was another old Kings Cross Police Station, which was built in 1842 and still stands on Kings Cross Road, sandwiched between the present-day Kings Cross Police

King's Cross
Police Station,
King's
Cross Road,
London WC1
(1870–c. 1992).

Station on one side and the old Clerkenwell Magistrates' Court on the other. All three buildings are Grade II listed.

The Magistrates' Court was designed by John Dixon Butler and dates from 1906. It has fine orange brick to the upper storeys and elaborate Portland stone dressings and a Welsh-slate mansard roof and is in a Free-Classical/Arts and Crafts/Queen Anne Revival style.[34]

The police station opened in 1870 and was designed by Thomas Charles Sorbey, Surveyor to the Metropolitan Police. It is made from stock bricks with Portland and Tilbury stone.[35] The present-day Kings Cross Police station is not open to the public.

It has been suggested that the 1842 police station was the work of Charles Reeves, Surveyor to the Metropolitan Police, but this is debatable as he did not take up his post until 1842 and the construction of the building had already started in February 1841.[36]

Muswell Hill Police Station

Freehold land was purchased at Fortis Green Road in 1899 for £2,500 and the new police station opened in 1904.[37] It has at times been known as Fortis Green Police Station as well as Muswell Hill Police Station. Police officer accommodation was usually provided by the station and an example of this is at Muswell Hill, where accommodation for one married Inspector was eight shillings per week, one married constable was four shillings and six pence per week, and ten unmarried constables were paid one shilling per week.[38] The Police Surveyor, John Dixon Butler, usually designed police accommodation buildings in a separate block adjacent or attached to the police station.[39]

In 1966 Muswell Hill Police Station was part of a programme in which some stations were closed on an experimental basis.[40] It was closed at night initially for a period of six months and the officers who were usually assigned to night duty were posted to other duties. A telephone was connected to the sub-divisional station and installed in a receptacle

Muswell Hill Police Station, 115 Fortis Green Road, Muswell Hill, N2 (1904–2013).

in the window of the station for members of the public, and for police as part of the Telephone Box System.[41] Arrangements had also been made with the G.P.O. for incoming public telephone calls to be diverted to Hornsey Station. The experiment was unsuccessful, and the station reopened at nights in April 1968.[42] The same kind of system of contacting police via a phone on the outside of the building (these days a yellow phone) has been reintroduced recently at some police buildings which were previously police stations manned with a front office, for example Southwark Police Station.

Muswell Hill front office closed in 2013 and the building was sold in 2014 for £3.5 million. It is now a 'luxury collection of 2, 3 and 4 bedroomed apartments and town houses, offering the perfect blend of London and village life. These stunning Edwardian period properties offer high ceilings'.[43]

In 2015 the Planet Organic Store in Muswell Hill was a 'police contact point' where the public could meet police and report crime. It was meant to receive crime reports, give advice to victims, process witness statements and deal with driving documents following road accidents.[44]

New Southgate Police Station

The site for New Southgate Police Station was purchased freehold in 1886 and three years later the station was operational. It is not clear exactly where it was located as Surveyors' maps have shown that it was at the junction of Garfield Road and Betstyle Road, but the road names were probably altered after the building of a large housing estate in the area. It was situated virtually opposite the local undertakers, A. Seawards ampersand Sons, which was at 138 High Road and that building has been converted into part of the adjacent Sikh temple. It would have been a busy high street during part of the nineteenth century and for most of the twentieth century, but by the 1980s it was no longer a through road and

New Southgate Police Station, 151 Garfield Road, New Southgate, N11 (1889–1990).

had become a small road with one pub and a few small grocery type stores. When the photograph of New Southgate Police Station was taken recently the pub had gone and the undertakers had relocated to a nearby busier road.

A hut on wheels was erected in the police station yard to house a fire hose and the hut was extended in 1909 and 1929, but by 1930 the use of the hut by the Southgate Local Board for fire safety was no longer needed and Special Constables used it instead.[45]

Like other police stations in the Metropolitan Police area, such as Muswell Hill, it was closed in December 1960 for an experimental period of six months while night duty officers were posted elsewhere. A telephone was connected to the sub-divisional station and installed in a pillar near the front door for use by the public. By 1968 the police station was only operating limited hours as a police office and the area was policed as a neighbourhood unit by Southgate Police Station. However, the building was still used by various squads and units until 1990 when it was closed and later sold and converted into flats.

St John's Wood Police Station

There is a record of a police station in St John's Wood in 1864, but towards the end of the century land was purchased at New Street from the trustees of the Will of William Henry Cavendish Scott, the 4th Duke of Portland, and a new police station was opened in 1896.[46] It was known as Portland Town Police Station. By the start of the First World War it had been renamed St John's Wood, as the name of Portland Town was found to be confusing for members of the public because they could not find the police station telephone number in the phone directory. There were also problems with the delivery of letters and parcels as some items were sent to Portland in Dorset in error.[47] The building was sold in 2013 for £8.5 million.

38

St John's Wood Police Station, New Street, St John's Wood, London NW8 (1896–c. 2013).

Second World War air raid siren on top of St John's Wood Police Station, New Street, St John's Wood, London NW8 (1896–c. 2013).

Tottenham Police Station

Although Tottenham Police Station was not scheduled to close, there was the ominous sign of a yellow phone outside the station and an online comment that the twenty-four-hour access station was closed when someone wanted to report a crime, so it may have either closed or reduced opening hours recently. However, it has been included in this book as I am Tottenham born and can trace ancestry in Tottenham back to the mid-eighteenth century. My ancestors lived virtually in the shadow of the local parish church and my great-grandfather, with Irish ancestry, helped to build the Catholic Church. The Church

Tottenham Police Station, 398 High Road, Tottenham Haringey (1914–present day).

used to face a public house and the Co-op undertakers on the High Road, but these are now both closed to make room for the new Tottenham Hotspur football ground which now dwarfs the church.

The land for a police station was purchased freehold in 1859, but by 1910 the area had good transport links into central London and had become increasingly urbanised and industrialised, with a population increase to almost 149,000. By this time the police station was deemed to be too small, dirty and dilapidated and when the Commissioner, Sir Edward Henry, visited on 30 August 1910 he commented in the Occurrence Book that the 'accommodation here – residential and administrative is inadequate and unsatisfactory'.[48] In 1911 there were plans to buy the adjacent property at 394–396 High Road and it was purchased for £1,500, with the new police station opening in 1914. The building was modernised in the 1970s and 1990s.

The stables I used to pass on my way to school and where my sister used to feed the police horses with apples have gone and they are now a new extension building. The stables had been used for over 100 years, but the last horses at the stables, Steve, Trojan, Sultan and Statesman, were taken out on their last beat on 31 March 1995 to the band of the Coldstream Guards. Chief Superintendent David Gilbertson said the horses would be missed by many people as the stable horses 'have become an institution over the years and it is a shame they are going. Police Officers and local people have become used to seeing them around'.[49]

There is a memorial outside Tottenham Police Station to PC William Frederick Tyler, who along with a young boy called Ralph Joscelyne, were murdered in 1909 during the Tottenham Outrage. This was a chase across North London by members of the public and the police chasing two armed robbers, who were members of the Latvian Socialist Party and shot at the people pursuing them.

Tottenham
(St Ann's
Road), 289
St Ann's Road,
Tottenham,
Haringey,
(1885–c. 2001).

Tottenham (St Ann's Road Police Station)

Land was purchased in 1884 at Woodberry Down for a police station to be erected and it was opened in 1885.[50] A fire engine was also kept on standby in the station yard.[51] Just before the Second World War a District Garage was built on land at the station and there was also a large workshop to deal with the repair and maintenance of vehicles, reflecting the increasing use of motor vehicles by the police. The station was still open to the public in 1998 but by 2001 it was no longer used to charge prisoners.[52] The old police station has now been extended along the side road called Hermitage Road and the building has been converted into flats but has kept the original front façade.

Whetstone Police Station

The original police station was approximately 200 yards away from the present one and situated in the High Road with the freehold purchased in 1851, but by 1911 the police station was deemed unsuitable. The Surveyor's report into the condition of Metropolitan police stations in 1881 said that Whetstone had a well which had become polluted.[53] A new site in Friern Barnet Lane was obtained. Although the adjacent premises at 1170–1172 High Road, formerly 1 Friern Barnet Lane, were bought in 1948 the new police station did not open until 1960.[54] In 1972 Spike Milligan contacted the Metropolitan Police for information about the police station history and the existence and location of old stabling for the Horse Patrols.[55]

41

Whetstone Police Station, 170 High Road, Whetstone, Barnet, N20 (1889–2013).

Whetstone Police Station closed its front counter in 2013 and the building was sold for just over £4 million. The 1960s building still stands, but now has an extension and has been converted into a school.

Willesden Police Station

A freehold site was purchased for £1,200 by the Receiver for the Metropolitan Police in 1892 and was on the site of the old 'Willesden House', which was situated at the corner of Huddlestone Road and Willesden Lane.[56] The police station was designed by John Dixon

Willesden Police Station, 96 High Road, Willesden Green, NW10 (1896–2013).

Butler and opened in 1896. In 1956 the town clerk wrote to Scotland Yard to ask whether they wanted to build a new police station in a proposed Civic Centre in the High Road, but the Commissioner decided that the location of the building would not be central enough.[57] In 2012 the Mayor of London was asked whether Willesden Green Police Station was going to be closed down and he answered that 'it is on the disposal list for 2012/2013. However final approval for its disposal has yet to be given. I can assure you that in line with my Mayoral priority no front counter will be closed without a new improved facility being put in its place'.[58]

In 1995 the station was awarded a trophy for the large garden category in the Metropolitan Police gardens competition.[59]

Winchmore Hill Police Station

The site bought for Winchmore Hill Police Station in Green Lanes was originally part of the Highfield House estate, but later owned by the London Brick Company.[60] Highfield House was a red brick house built after 1865 and the land around this house and nearby Eaton Villa was sold off in plots.[61] The police station was designed by John Dixon Butler and opened in 1915. It has a dated commemorative engraved stone near the front entrance, which seems to be typical of the style of Edwardian detail added to the front of many police stations. It is a Grade II listed building of red brick and consists of three storeys.[62]

The front counter closed in 2013 and the building was sold the following year for £900,000. There are planning proposals to convert the building to residential use. It has been recognised that the flats must embody the police station in size and in design, although the cells and custodial interior will be an architectural challenge. The present plans look basic and uninspired and they should not 'just be plonked down where there is a space'.[63]

Winchmore Hill Police Station, 687 Green Lanes, Winchmore Hill, Enfield, N21 (1915–*c.* 2013).

CHAPTER 4

South London Police Stations

Battersea Police Station

In 1858 land became available for purchase to build a purpose-built police station in Battersea. It was near the Castle Public House and situated at the corner of Hyde Road (later Hyde Lane) and Battersea Bridge Road. The new building was designed by Charles Reeves and opened in 1861. It was a compact, stock-brick building of two storeys over a basement and embellished by the incised word POLICE over the round-headed door.[1]

Battersea Police Station, Battersea Bridge Road, Wandsworth, SW11 (1907–2013).

In 1901 there were reports of drainage problems at the station as the Thames flooded into the building, along with sewage, and a number of police officers caught diphtheria and typhoid.[2] In 1907 a new property was purchased at 112–118 Battersea Bridge Road and a new station was built by F. G. Minter, Contractors of Putney, and designed by John Dixon Butler. It was usual at that time to incorporate section house accommodation within the police station and at Battersea it was provided for single police officers. There was also one set of married quarters.[3] The police station was closed in 2013, sold for £6 million and has since been refurbished with an extension to provide residential flats.

Poignantly Battersea Police Station decided to hold a closing day event: 'Battersea Police Station: An Invitation to the last Open Day'.[4] It seems to have been common for Metropolitan Police Stations to quietly close its doors for the last time with little interaction and communication with the community. Likely reasons for this lack of publicity are probably policy-driven, prompted by the belief that the less attention drawn to the widespread closures is a better option and any closing day events might be viewed by the public as a waste of time, money and manpower by the police.

Beckenham Police Station

Beckenham Police Station was opened in 1833 to cope with an increase in robberies in the area but replaced by a new building in 1885.[5] In the Metropolitan Police Heritage Centre there is an illustration of the original brick Beckenham cage which was demolished but had been used to hold prisoners before the Metropolitan Police policed the area.[6] The police station was closed down in 2010. In April 2018 part of the building was being used as a beauty spa and another part of the building was a cocktail bar.

Above and right: Beckenham Police Station, High Street, Beckenham, Bromley, BR3 (1885–2010).

Camberwell Police Station, Church Street, Southwark, SE5 (1898–2019).

Camberwell Police Station

The first reference to police premises in Camberwell is when the 'Old Cage' for holding prisoners situated next to 'The Joiners' Arms' in Camberwell High Road was handed back to the parish authorities in 1848.[7] The station had been preceded by a watch house, which was known as the Round House, and may have been the last of London's oldest watch houses. It was actually described as a police station rather than a watch house in 1820 because it had been extended by additional leasing of the adjacent houses.[8]

In 1858 a house next door to the police station was rented on a lease for fifty years with the proviso that cells were built within by the owner. The freehold was purchased in 1887 and was described as two old houses adapted for police use.[9] A freehold site at 22 Church Street was purchased for £4,000 and the new police station opened in 1898.[10] It was designed by John Dixon Butler in red brick in Flemish bond with stone dressings.[11] The police station closed its doors for the last time in March 2019 when Camberwell police officers invited the public via social media to come in and say goodbye.

Croydon Police Station

Croydon Police Station was designed by John Butler and opened in 1895 but demolished in 1980. It was replaced by a park opened by Queen Elizabeth II in 1983 and called Queen's Gardens.

The 1895 police station had been preceded by a building at 13 North End Road which had been used as Wilson's Tea Rooms and then as a shop called Kennards.[12]

Queen's
Gardens,
Croydon, CR9.

Deptford Police Station

A police station was in existence in Deptford by 1857 but was replaced by a new station in 1912. It was located in an area of poverty, disease and slum housing with a high crime level, which led the Divisional Superintendent to comment that 'the conditions of the inhabitants round about was very poor, casual and in chronic want. It was a resort of bad characters, and many crimes of a serious nature happened occasionally in the district and were to be expected'.[13]

Deptford Police Station was located at 116 Amersham Vale and designed by John Dixon Butler. It is a Grade II listed building and consists of three storeys, basement and

Deptford
Police Station,
Amersham Vale,
New Cross,
Lewisham, SE14
(1912–2017).

high-pitched tiled roof with end chimneys. There is a wrought iron handrail and area railings framing a white stone plinth with the date '1912' and a lamp holder of cast and wrought iron above it.[14] It was closed down in 2017 and there have been plans to demolish and build new flats, but at the present time it is still being used as artists' studios. The planning proposals note that the cells still exist but there is some debate as to whether the tiling is original or later. There are also original doors, screens, parquet flooring, tiling, rails and stairs and more.[15]

In 1905 two young men broke into a shop in Deptford and battered the owner and his wife to death. They were convicted at the Old Bailey of murder but the identification of a fingerprint on the cash box was instrumental in getting a guilty verdict. This was the first-time fingerprint identification had been successfully used in a conviction. It was probable that they were held in the existing cells at Deptford Police Station following their arrest.

Greenwich Police Station

In 1822 a cage to house prisoners was erected on the Greenwich Road at the corner with Cut Throat Lane. In 1836 a fifty-year lease was purchased to build a purpose-built police station at Blackheath Road and after the freehold was purchased in 1899, a new station was constructed and opened in 1910.[16]

It was designed by John Dixon Butler in a free Classical Style and consisted of a Magistrates' Court with the police station in the same building and the Royal Coat of Arms was carved in stone by Lawrence Turner. The police station had a mosaic tiled floor with the M. P. monogram. The leaded lights in the hall are glazed with coloured glass by William Morris ampersand Sons.[17] It is now closed down and plans are being submitted to develop it as a hotel.

Greenwich Police Station, Blackheath Road, Greenwich, SE10 (1910–1962).

48

Kew Police Station,
North Road, Kew,
Richmond, TW9
(1914–1933).

Kew Police Station

Kew Police Station at 96 North Road opened in 1912 but was closed in 1933 as part of a reorganisation under the Commissioner Lord Trenchard 1931–1933. Trenchard had been nicknamed 'The Father of the Air Force' as he had re-established the RAF, devising everything for the new service. After retirement he had taken on the role of Commissioner of the Metropolitan Police and introduced sweeping reforms, such as improvements in wireless communication, information, police housing and canteen facilities during his short tenure.[18]

Kingston Police Station

Premises were leased in 1840 in the London Road to use for police purposes and the old watch house was handed back to the parish authorities in 1841.[19] Another new police station was opened in 1864 at 6 Old London Road, Kingston, and replaced in 1968 by the present police station. The old 1864 building is a Grade II listed building and in July 2018 it was being used as offices with the name 'Kopshop'.

In 1912 the Commissioner wrote to the Receiver requesting a new building as conditions were very poor at the station.[20] The following year the Divisional Surgeon also submitted a report on the sanitary conditions of the police station and stated, 'The Inspector's office has no ventilation and at times the atmosphere is suffocating'. He goes on to say that he was called to see a prisoner the previous evening and the conditions were so bad that he found it sickening and 'quite unfit for any human being to be shut up in the cells as they are badly constructed and not at all up to the modern requirements'.[21] The police station was also used for police housing and he reported that the Inspector's children are 'often ailing and with enlarged glands, discharge and inflamed throats'.[22]

Kingston had a lot of difficulties in setting up a new police station as, although a site had been purchased in 1914, by the end of the war it was already found to be unsuitable for the needs of the police. Another site was found, and the purchase was about to be concluded

Kingston Police Station,
High Road, Kingston, KT2
(1864–1968).

when the Second World War started.[23] In 1951 attempts to purchase the same site were restarted. However, there were issues with town planning and the purchase was again delayed. It eventually went ahead and almost reached the completion stage before town planning again prevented completion. A new site was purchased in 1965.[24] The Metropolitan Police again faced problems as this site was not only adjoining the old Guildhall and the ancient Coronation stone, but it was also very wet land. This time, however, the new police station went ahead and opened in 1968 and is currently open twenty-four hours a day.

Lee Road Police Station

The Bow Street Patrol, formed in 1805 by Sir Richard Ford, had a station in Lee Green, but following the formation of the Metropolitan Police and an Act of 1839, which extended the area that the Metropolitan Police covered to include Lee, a new police station was planned there.[25] It was built at 258a Lee Road in 1850 on land leased from Lord Northbrook.[26] By the end of the century Lee's population had greatly increased and the site's freehold was purchased along with the house next door which was known as 'Ivy Cottage'. A new police station was opened in 1903, with it being renumbered in 1909 as 418 Lee High Road.[27]

It is a Grade II listed two storey building of red brick with stone dressings designed by John Dixon Butler. The police station was fumigated in 1939 as C.I.D. had seized stolen bed linen from a local pawnbroker's shop which was bug infested.[28] It was again fumigated the following year after a louse infestation in one of the cells, and in 1948 there was a mouse problem in the food store of the canteen. As one author points out, Lee Road was no different to other police stations in London when dealing with some prisoners and property which was not clean.[29] The police station closed down in 2003 and is now residential flats.

Lee Road Police
Station, Lee Green,
Lewisham, SE12
(1903–2003).

Lewisham Police Station

The first police station at Lewisham is believed to be on the site where Marks & Spencers now stands, with the second police station, which until 1817 had been the old parish workhouse, adjacent to John Thackeray's Almshouses.[30] Before the Metropolitan Police policed the area there was a small octagonal building on Watch House Green, called the Lewisham Cage, to hold petty offenders, but some prisoners set fire to their straw bedding and died before the key to the Cage could be found.[31]

A new purpose-built police station designed by John Dixon Butler was opened in 1899 and is a Grade II listed building. A letter from the Receiver to the Surveyor of the Metropolitan Police, dated 13 February 1897, points out that the corridor and divisions between the cells are only 9 inches thick, the outer walls only 14 inches thick and that the cells are not provided with guard bars. 'These things are not allowed in County Stations,

Lewisham Police
Station, Ladywell
Road, Lewisham, SE13
(1899–2004).

but they have hitherto been approved by the Secretary of State for the Metropolitan Police Stations'. It was later agreed that Commissioner Sir E. Henderson thought 14 inches sufficiently thick for Metropolitan Police Stations if prisoners were only confined in the cells for one night.[32]

It has been sold and has been converted into private flats and a local pub, owned by the Wetherspoon chain of public houses, and has been renamed 'The Watch House'.

In 2004 a new police station to cover Lewisham was opened at a new site and at the present time is the most modern and up-to-date station in Europe. It was built in partnership between the Metropolitan Police and the private sector with the aim of replacing old police stations and providing stations more equipped to deal with modern policing.[33] The partner provides the building and services and maintains it on a contract for twenty-five years. After this period the police station remains the property of the private company.[34]

New Malden Police Station

A freehold site near the new railway station was bought for £600 in 1887 and New Malden Police Station opened shortly afterwards. It was closed in 1998 and is now a Wetherspoon pub called 'The Watchman' but has retained the police station metal cell doors. The Wetherspoon chain often provides a brief local history of the area or famous residents who have entered the pages of history. They have several public houses nationally which were old police stations and information is displayed with photographs and text.

A memorial garden outside the pub is dedicated to PC Frederick Atkins who died in the line of duty on 23 September 1881, aged twenty-three. He was shot in nearby Kingston Hill by a burglar and was taken back to Kingston Police Station but died later that day. 1,500 police officers attended his funeral.

New Malden Police Station, New Malden, Kingston KT3 (1881–1998).

Peckham Police Station, Peckham High Street, Southwark, SE15 (1893–present day).

Peckham Police Station

A property known as 'The Clock House' in the high street was leased from 1847 to 1903 for use as the police station.[35] By the 1880s the building was thought to be unsuitable for its present needs and the Metropolitan Police made a compulsory purchase of the property in 1890, with the property owner awarded £4,000 compensation by the High Court.[36] In 1893 a new building, designed by John Butler, was opened on the same site and in 1988 the station was refurbished and reopened this time by H.R.H. Princess Alexandra. The police station was listed as closed in 2017 but apparently is still open to the public.

Penge Police Station

Home Office approval for a police station at Penge was given in 1868 and a year later a Mr William Gibson of the Parochial Offices, Anerley Road, wrote to the Commissioner urging the building of a police station as winter was coming and there would be increased

Penge Police Station, High Street, Bromley, SE20 (1872–2010).

crime, growing poverty and unemployment of the lower classes.[37] He pointed out that the Hamlet of Penge paid £3,000 a year to the Metropolitan Police and had been begging for a police station for three years.[38] A temporary police station was opened in 1870, followed by a permanent building in 1872, which remained open until 2010. The freehold was sold in 2011 for £625,000 and it is now a college with a number of private residences in the old police yard called Old Police Station Mews.

Richmond Police Station

The old watch house was replaced by a new building in 1841 but by 1867 a new site was obtained facing onto George Street. The new station was opened in 1871 and was, in turn, replaced by a new purpose-built police station on freehold land at Red Lion Street in 1912.[39] The police station

Richmond Police Station, Red Lion Street, Richmond, TW9 (1912–2013).

Richmond Police Station, Sovereign Place, Richmond, TW9 (2013–c. 2019).

was closed down in 2013. It has been partly demolished, although the front façade has been retained and it has a rear extension. It is now residential housing and a restaurant. Kew Police Station closed in 1932 and Richmond has since policed Kew.[40] A new police station was built near Richmond railway and Underground station at Sovereign Gate and opened within the last ten years but has now been sold and the building is used for offices.

Rotherhithe Police Station

An early police station was in use from 1838 at 23 Paradise Street in Southwark. It is a Grade II listed building and it is now called Sir William Gaitskell House after its first occupant. The actual building dates from 1814 and it still has the cast-iron handrail, overthrow with lamp-holder and area railings.

In 1881 the brass lion-shaped door knockers to the police station were stolen but turned up again in 1952 after a death bed confession by a man to his daughter saying that he had taken them as a drunken dare and kept them hidden since![41] The police station was closed down in 2013 and is now in private use.

Rotherhithe
Police Station,
Paradise Street,
Southwark,
SE16
(1836–1965).

Southwark Police Station, Borough High Street, Southwark, SE1 (1940–present day).

Southwark Police Station

The first purpose-built police station in Southwark was opened in 1844 in Montague Street, Stones End, and was designed by Charles Reeves. Montague Street still exists but has been renamed Stones End Street and runs parallel to Borough High Street. A new police station, designed by Frederick Caiger, was opened in 1870 in Blackman Street (since renamed Borough High Street) and is the site of the current Southwark Police Station. In 1920 property at 323 Borough High Street and adjacent properties were purchased to enable extension of the station and the new station opened in 1940.[42] In 1958 a bronze plaque was erected: 'Here was 'Stones End' where 'Town Street' met the old Turnpike Road one of the parliamentary forts, erected to defend London during the civil war, stood here'.[43] The front office is apparently still open, but with limited opening hours and a contact phone placed outside.

Streatham Police Station

Streatham Police Station opened in 1868, but by 1908 there were plans to rebuild the station. A memo was sent from the Commissioner to the Receiver saying that the rebuilding should be a priority, as the previous building was forty years old, and unsuitable, as Streatham was no longer a village.[44] The old post office was purchased, and the station was situated on the High Road at the junction with Shrubbery Road. It was designed by John Dixon Butler and opened in 1912. It had three storeys and was designed as a cube. At the third-floor level the stone cornice was used to create a large stone pediment as a decorative device on the three visible sides of the building, and a commemorative foundation stone was laid by the main door in Shrubbery Road.[45]

The station provided accommodation for both married and single officers and the policy had been to house police officers in the same or adjacent buildings even until the 1960s

Streatham Police Station, High Road,
Streatham, Lambeth, SW16 (1912–2013).

and 1970s. For example, Brentford Police Station, which was opened in 1967, had a large section house for officers and Marylebone Police Station, opened in 1977, was built with an adjacent building for police accommodation.

Additional land was bought in the 1960s for an extension to Streatham Police Station. The front office closed in 2017 and has since been sold for over £4 million. Planning applications for residential accommodation and a mews block extension in the old police yard, as was the case at Penge Police Station, have been proposed.

Tooting Police Station

In 1864 Tooting Police Station had one sergeant, fourteen police constables and one horse.[46] The present station was opened in 1939 and designed by G. Mackenzie Trench, Police Chief Architect and Surveyor. The site was about 150 yards away from the previous station which had consisted of an old house which was known as 'The Golf House'.[47] The new station included a section house for eighty single officers and twelve flats for married officers and their families.

A Freedom of Information request stated that the front office closed down in 2017 but in late 2019 their website showed that the station had limited opening hours.

An Inspector from Tooting Police Station wrote in the Police Station Occurrence Book that he had attended H. M. Prison, Wandsworth, for the inquest of Lord Haw-Haw, William Joyce where the jury returned a verdict that 'William Joyce died on 3 January 1946 from injury to the brain and spinal column consequent upon judicial hanging'.[48]

Tooting Police Station often won prizes for the upkeep of the station garden, winning the annual prize in 1971. In 1976 their hard work was destroyed by a drunken man who tore up ten shrubs and threw one of them at a police officer who had come out of the station to see what was happening.[49]

Tooting Police Station, Mitcham Road, Tooting, Wandsworh, SW17 (1939–present day).

Tower Bridge Police Station

Tower Bridge Police Station and Magistrates' Court became operational in 1904 and was designed by John Dixon Butler in an Edwardian Baroque Style, and is now a Grade II listed building. It closed in 1999 and is now a hotel called 'The Dixon Hotel' named after John Dixon Butler.[50]

Tower Bridge Police Station, Tooley Street, Southwark, SE1 (1904–1999).

Wandsworth Police Station,
Trinity Road, Wandsworth,
SW17 (1883–2011).

Wandsworth Common (Trinity Road) Police Station

Trinity Road Police Station at Wandsworth was near Tooting Bec and was built about 1890, constructed using a plum brick and had a stone door-case.

It was amalgamated with Earlsfield Police Station and changed to Police Office, rather than Police Station, status in 1974. It was closed in 2011, sold in 2014 for £1.5 million and has been converted into residential flats and office space. Adjacent new houses which must have been on land owned by the Metropolitan Police are called Peel House, Rowan House (named after the first joint Commissioner of the Metropolitan Police) and Bow House.

Wimbledon Police Station

There has been a police presence in Wimbledon as far back as 1790 and in 1804 local shopkeepers and some wealthy households agreed to pay for a Wimbledon Watch to patrol the streets. There have been a number of police stations in Wimbledon before the current building was opened in 1900. It was refurbished in 1937 and again in 1987.[51]

It was one of the police stations announced for closure by the London Mayor, Sadiq Khan, in 2017, but strong local opposition to the closure brought the case to the High Court. Paul Kohler, who was the victim of a violent attack in Wimbledon, took the case

Wimbledon Police Station, Queens Road, Wimbleden, SE19 (1900–present day).

to the High Court as he believed that his life had been saved by the attendance of police from nearby Wimbledon Police Station, who arrived within eight minutes of the 999 telephone call. Mr Kohler lost the wider case challenging the closure of more than half of the police stations that were scheduled to close, but it was ruled that the decision to close Wimbledon Police Station was unlawful and must be reconsidered. Various options are under discussion to keep the station open.

In 1963 a young couple on their wedding day found that due to a mix up in their guest house booking they had nowhere to stay and went to Wimbledon Police Station, where the station sergeant turned the waiting room into a bedroom for them. A document was apparently supplied to them to say they had spent their first night of marriage at Wimbledon Police Station, but as there was no official record that it happened the police refused to comment to the press.[52]

Woolwich Old Dockyard Police Station

The station was built *c.* 1841 in Church Street to police the dockyards but closed a few years later and the station was relocated in Woolwich. The old police station still exists and is a Grade II listed building now used as offices. It consists of two storeys and is made of stock brick in Flemish bond with stone dressings and has a commemoration stone dated 1843 on the hopper, two large bridge-like chimneys and two stone porches[53]

Woolwich Dock Police Station, William Street, Greenwich, SE10 (*c.* 1841).

Chapter 5

East London Police Stations

Arbour Square Police Station, Whitechapel

In 1841 land was rented from the Mercers' Company for the building of Thames Police Court at Arbour Square and a police station was also built on this site.[1] In 1888 the land freehold was bought, and the building was updated in the 1920s, but was damaged in 1944 by a V1 Flying Bomb.[2] The front counter was closed in 1999 and both the court and the police station have been sold and refurbished into residential flats.[3]

Arbour Square Police Station, East Arbour Street, Tower Hamlets, E1 (1923–1999).

Barking Police Station, Ripple Road, Barking, IG11 (1910–2013).

Barking Police Station

The first Metropolitan Police station in Barking was built in 1849 at a cost of £942 and a new purpose-built police station opened in 1910 at 4 Ripple Road, Barking.[4]

During the 1980s prison officers' dispute, prisoners who were on remand and had not been convicted were housed at various police stations and some prisoners liked Barking so much that they wrote thank you letters for the hospitality. One prisoner wrote that

> I can only say that during my short stay in Barking I saw a side to the police force which completely changed my opinion of people who wear uniforms. It's a pity that so many people on my side of the fence couldn't have shared this with me. Could you please express my thanks to the people concerned for the kindness shown.[5]

The front counter at Barking Police Station was closed and the building was sold in 2014 for £925,000. It has been refurbished and is now residential flats. Following the closure of the station and before the building was sold over thirty people were found to be living illegally in the building.

Barkingside Police Station

People living in Barkingside wanted a new police station in the area and in 1869 the freehold for a beer house called the Mossford Arms was purchased and converted into a police station which opened in 1872.[6] The freehold to the adjoining properties was also bought, but the station became unsuitable as times changed. A new one was built which opened in 1964 and was on the same site.[7] The new building was constructed using unsuitable glass material which made it a hot building to work in. There was little privacy internally and it was eventually refurbished in the 1990s. It was scheduled for closure but was still open in late 2018.

In 1989 ex-detective Rodney Whitchelo was convicted for a series of blackmails involving the contamination of Heinz food in supermarkets. It was reported in the media that he was based at Barkingside Police Station, as part of the Reginal Crime Squad, but he would actually have been based at another police building where the Squad operated from.[8]

Barkingside Police Station, 1 High Street, Barkingside, Redbridge (1993–present day).

Bethnal Green Police Station

The existing Bethnal Green Police Station in Victoria Park Square is not planned to close. The previous Bethnal Green police station has been included as it is an example of how errors were sometimes made when the new Metropolitan Police Force organised the location of its new police stations.[9]

In 1860 land was purchased to build a police station at 243 Bethnal Green Road. Nine years later more land was purchased at 458 Bethnal Green Road to build another police station.[10] This meant that the Metropolitan Police ended up with two police stations in separate divisions which were situated less than 1-mile apart. Moreover, Leman Street, Commercial Road and Shoreditch Police Stations were also very nearby, but it could be argued that the East End was a lively area associated with a high crime level and probably benefited from the police cells and extra police presence in the area. Even as late as the 1980s a police officer stationed at Bethnal Green estimated that the division had about 132 pubs alone on its ground to keep it busy.[11]

In 1894 Bethnal Green station at 243 Bethnal Green Road was rebuilt but it closed down in 1994 when it was relocated to the new station at 12 Victoria Park Square, London. Nearby Leman Street Police Station was also closed down and transferred to the new police station at Victoria Park Square.

The relocation was described as: 'Two East End stations synonymous with the Victorian era of policing merge into a new building'.[12] Also reported in the same newspaper was PC Harry Harris, who had spent his fifty-year career at Bethnal Green, who summed it up as

> We are saying goodbye to a lovely-looking building, well-proportioned and full of memories. Refurbishments have destroyed the interior I remember – there were brown tiles with a row of green tiles, fireplaces, gleaming brass and generally a homely feel.[13]

An emergency air raid shelter, which was owned by the British United Shoe Machinery Company and used during the Second World War, actually had its exit in the police station yard and was not blocked up until 1948.[14]

The old Bethnal Green Police Station was not far from Bethnal Green tube station, which was the site of the 1943 tube tragedy and the worst civilian disaster of the Second World War, when 173 people were killed and nearly 100 people were injured. During an air raid attack a woman carrying a young child fell on the steps as she was going down to

Bethnal Green Road Police Station, Bethnal Green Road, Tower Hamlets, E2 (1894–1995).

the tube station shelter and was crushed by other people who fell on her unaware of what had happened. A general crush followed, but the tragedy was hushed up in the media as the government did not want public morale to fail. A memorial called 'The Stairway to Heaven' is in a nearby park to those who died in the tragedy, and there is an annual service to remember those who died and were injured.

There were investigations into the criminal activities of the Kray brothers at Bethnal Green Police Station, and it was also the station from which officers were sent to meet Winston Churchill at the nearby Siege of Sidney Street in the search for 'Peter the Painter'.[15]

The TV series *Maisie Raine*, starring Pauline Quirke, was filmed at the closed down station. Some local people thought that the police station had reopened, but criminals knew better and there were a series of break-ins at the building. There were so many that the production accountant got so frustrated that he used superglue to stick a one-pound coin to the carpet only to find that it had been removed by the following morning.[16] The police station was closed in 1995 and is used by a local business now.

Bow Police Station

In 1845, there was a police station and section house in Devons Lane, Bromley-by-Bow, which was replaced by a purpose-built station in 1860 at 116b Bow Road, E3, designed by Charles Reeves.[17]

It is now used as a funeral director's business called C. Selby. In 1913 Sylvia Pankhurst was arrested for breaking a window after a suffragette meeting in Bromley High Street, and strangely enough the window belonged to the same C. Selby who was located there at that time.[18] The old police station at 116b Bow Road was also opposite the club owned by the Kray Twins at 145 Bow Road.[19]

After Sylvia Pankhurst broke the window, she was taken to the new Bow Road Police Station which had opened in 1903.[20] The police station and the stables are Grade II listed

64

Above left: Bow Police Station, 111 Bow Road, Bow, Tower Hamlets, E3 (1903–2013).

Above right: Old Bow Police Station, 116b Bow Road, Bow, Tower Hamlets, E3 (1860–*c*. 1903).

buildings. The station was designed by John Dixon Butler in a Neo-Baroque style, with the stables designed at a later date by the interwar police surveyor Gilbert Mackenzie Trench (1885–1979) in a Modern style in white concrete.[21] It closed in 2013.

It has the characteristic triangle pediment above the stone porch with a lintel inscribed with the word 'Police' and a date stone adjacent to the porch.[22] Inside the building there are a number of original panelled doors and an original staircase with its iron balustrade and handrail. The lavatory block retains the original white glazed brick walls and there are eight cells and one communal cell. The stables retain their original stalls, skylight and floor surfaces.

Brick Lane Police Office

Brick Lane Police Office was opened about forty years ago as a result of racial tensions in the area. It has been included although the building is of no historical interest and had no aesthetic features. It was known as 'the hut' by police officers as it was virtually a portacabin.[23]

It is included because it is an example of a small police office where members of the public could attend the station if they needed to speak to the police. It provided a police presence in the area and local community, even though it did not have facilities for charging or holding prisoners, but was closed down in 2017.

An ex-Metropolitan police officer wrote about his time at Bethnal Green and said that his best time was working at Brick Lane, as it was a groundbreaking idea to take the Metropolitan Police into the local community at a period of tension, and that by being there over a period of time they built up links and trust within the local community.[24] Brick Lane Police Office closed in 2017.

In the early part of this century a large number of similar small police offices were opened by the Metropolitan Police. These days contact with local police is encouraged through the local Safer Neighbourhood Police Teams.

Brick Lane, Police Office, Brick Lane, Whitechapel, Tower Hamlets, E1 (*c.* 1980s–2017).

Chadwell Heath Police Station

Police Orders of 1864 noted that there was a Chadwell Heath Police Station which was a converted house, but the location is not known.[25] In 1890 freehold land in High Road at the junction with Station Road was purchased and a new police station was opened in 1892, closing when a new police station was opened in 1969 at Wangey Road, Chadwell Heath.[26]

The old police station is now a Wetherspoon pub called The Eva Hart, which is the name of a local woman who was one of the longest living survivors from the Titanic disaster. The 1960s Chadwell Police Station in Wangey Road is now a mosque.

Chadwell Heath Police Station, High Road, Chadwell Heath, Redbridge, RM6 (1892–1969).

Commercial Street Police Station,
160 Commercial Street, Tower Hamlets,
E1 (1876–1970).

Commercial Street Police Station

After the formation of the Metropolitan Police Force in 1829, an early watch house at Spital Square was probably still being used in 1862 by the Metropolitan Police, but a new purpose-built police station was opened in 1876 on nearby Commercial Street at the junction with Fleur-de-Lis Street. It was an unusually shaped building as it was on an odd plot of land and police officers stationed there referred to it as 'Comical Street'. It is a Grade II listed building, designed by F. G. Cougier and built using red brick with stone dressings.[27] It closed in 1970 and is now residential flats.

The 1881 census shows that Inspector Frederick George Abberline, who was later at the centre of the 'Jack the Ripper' investigation, was living at Commercial Street Police section house.[28]

Dagenham Police Station

Dagenham Police Station in Rainham Road South was built in the mid-nineteenth century and is a Grade II listed building. It was refurbished in 1937 and used until 1961 when a new police station was built nearby. It is now private flats.

Dagenham Police Station, High Road,
Dagenham, RM10 (c. 1850–1961).

East Ham Police Station,
4 High Street, Newham,
E6 (1904–2013).

East Ham Police Station

In 1862 an old police station at East Ham was demolished by the parish authorities without the permission of the Receiver of the Metropolitan Police.[29] A new police station designed by John Dixon Butler was opened in 1904 and was built in red brick, with Portland stone dressings and bands and a slate roof.[30] In 1937 it was rebuilt, and a new Section House was erected, but most of the existing building facing the high street was retained.[31] The front office closed in 2013 and it was sold for £3.4 million.

Hackney Police Station

Hackney has had a number of police stations, with the first police house at Jerusalem Square, Hackney Church Street.[32] By 1884 there was a police station at 422 Mare Street.[33] The building had been extended in 1852 and had a basement where there was a scullery, locker rooms, a cooking room, a clothes room and four coal sheds. On the ground floor there was a charge room, library, parade room and three water closets. There was also a stable for four horses.[34]

Some police stations also had facilities to receive dead bodies. Old Hackney Police Station had a mortuary at the rear of the building, which the Metropolitan Police kept along with the Coroner's Office after the building was sold.[35]

At the start of the twentieth century a new site was sought to replace the old Victorian one, but although the Metropolitan Police obtained the freehold for 34 St John's Church Road and the leasehold for the adjacent building in 1900, the Young Women's Christian Association, who were the tenants, wanted compensation so an out-of-court settlement was made for £1,400 in 1902. Consequently, it was not until 1904 that the new building was opened. It was designed by John Dixon Butler and is a Grade II listed building in red brick with stone dressings and had a Windsor type lantern with blue glass inscribed 'Police'.[36]

Hackney Police Station, 2 Lower
Clapton Road, Hackney,
E5 (1904–2013).

Like some other police stations it was believed that the building had a ghost, believed to be that of a superintendent who had committed suicide in the station.[37]

In 1940 a police section house for Hackney police officers was hit by a High Explosive bomb but only one person was injured as it was still under construction.[38]

Hackney Police Station had a Roll of Honour plaque inscribed with the names of officers who had distinguished themselves on the Division. It was three panels of polished wood with paintings of Hackney Old Tower and a copy of a police badge, listing the name and rank of the officer and why they were listed. One name was a John Elliott, who, in 1891, plunged into a reservoir of water in full uniform to rescue a four-year-old boy.[39]

The police station closed in 2013 and was sold for £7.6 million. Planning permission has been submitted for a Muslim free school to use the building. Archaeology South East has been commissioned to carry out an archaeological survey of the site as Hackney Gravels (underlying the site) is rich in Palaeolithic material and may provide other archaeological finds.

Leman Street Police Station

Leman Street Police Station was based in Whitechapel and was initially designated the headquarters of H (Whitechapel Division), replacing an earlier station and old watch house which had been taken over by the Metropolitan Police in 1829.[40] The new station opened in 1891 and was built upon the site of the Garrick theatre which had been adjacent to the old

Leman Street
Police Station,
Leman Street,
Tower Hamlets,
E1 (1970–1995).

watch house.[41] The police station closed in 1967 and three years later it was replaced by a new building, which subsequently closed its front office in 1995 when officers from Leman Street were transferred to Bethnal Green.

The investigation into the 'Jack the Ripper' murders, which took place in the East End between 1888 and 1891, was based at Leman Street initially under the command of Detective Inspector Edmund Reid. The television series *Ripper Street* was loosely based around Detective Inspector Edmund Reid. Police officers based at Leman Street Police Station were also responsible for policing the Royal Mint.[42]

North Woolwich Police Station

A police station was erected at North Woolwich in 1873 followed by a new purpose-built building in 1904.[43] It stayed open throughout the Second World War but was badly damaged and suffered four casualties.[44] In early 2019 it was still an empty and closed building.

North Woolwich
Police Station,
Albert Road,
North Woolwich,
Newham,
E16 (1904–2013).

Old Street Police Station and Magistrates' Court, Old Street, Hackney, E1 (1906–1999).

Old Street Police Station

John Dixon Butler designed the police station and Magistrates' Court in Shoreditch which was opened in 1906 and is now a Grade II listed building. The building included accommodation for one inspector on the first floor and forty single men on the second and third floors and had a mess room, kitchen area and rooms for keeping uniforms clean and dry.[45] The separate areas between the court and the police station were rigorously separated internally. Court Number Two on the first floor was the main juvenile court for east London from *c.* 1909 to 1925.[46] The central entrance bay has a triangular pediment with the horizontal base recessed, which encloses a stone-carved Royal coat-of-arm. It has been described as one of the finest Edwardian civic buildings in London, accommodating courtrooms, station living quarters and cell blocks.[47] The police station closed in 1973. The whole building, including the court, was closed in approximately 1999 and the whole complex has been refurbished and is a luxury hotel.

This court saw the Krays appear for demanding 'money with menaces' and the playwright Joe Orton accused of stealing and defacing library books from Islington library.

Plaistow Police Station

In 1851 the old watch house, which was known as 'The Old Cage', was handed back to the parish authorities by the Metropolitan Police and in 1864 a new station was built in the Barking Road.[48] More freehold land was bought in the same road and although there were planning problems relating to height restrictions and specifications set into the covenants, the new police station was opened in 1912. The front counter was closed down in 2017.

Plaistow
Police Station,
444 Barking Road,
Plaistow, Newham,
E13 (1912–2017).

Walthamstow Police Station

Vestry House, Church End, Walthamstow, is now a museum, but in 1841 the police station was based in the building.[49] The internal lock-up cell can still be seen at the museum and has graffiti written on the walls by people held in the cells. On one occasion someone locked in a cell managed to demolish the roof and escape.[50]

In 1868 a new police station was opened at Lea Bridge Road, Walthamstow, and all police business was transferred from Vestry House.[51] Land was purchased at the corner of Clay Road (Forest Road) and Greenleaf Road and a new police station became operational in 1892. This building was reconstructed and extended in 1941, but the front counter closed in 2012 and the building was sold the following year for just over £1 million.

Between 1898 and 1906, complaints, which sound familiar today, were made by the Overseers of the Poor of the Parish of Walthamstow about the shortage of police in the area.[52] Walthamstow Police Station had a number of officers who sang with the J Division Male Voice Choir during the 1950s and they made an appearance on a BBC television variety show in 1958.[53]

Walthamstow
Police Station,
360 Forest Road,
Waltham Forest
E17 (1892–2012).

Wanstead
Police Station,
Spratt
Hall Road,
Wanstead,
Redbridge, E11
(1886–2013).

Wanstead Police Station

Wanstead Police Station in Spratt Hall Road was opened in 1886.[54] Wanstead closed its front counter in 2013 and was sold the following year for £1.6 million and has been converted into residential flats. On closure it still had its original cells, the stable stores and hay loft.[55]

Wapping Police Station

Although Wapping Police Station is not scheduled for closure it has been included in this book because it houses the Metropolitan Police Marine Unit, which has been recognised by UNESCO as the world's oldest continuously serving police force, having been formed in 1798. As it is based next to the River Thames and has policed the Thames and the immediate area around the docks for over 200 years it is part of the lifeblood of the history of London. It became part of the Metropolitan Police in 1839 and is now known as the Metropolitan Police Marine Unit, but in the past it has been called the Thames Division, River Police or Thames River Police. The station has always been based in Wapping high street and the present building is still an operational police station, but also has a museum attached to it relating to the history of the River Police. John Dixon Butler was the architect of the present police station which opened in 1910.

Wapping Police Station, 98 Wapping High Street, Tower Hamlets, E1 (1871–present day).

West Ham/Stratford Police Station

There was an early watch house and police station policing West Ham, but freehold land was purchased at 64–66 West Ham Lane and a new station opened in 1895. It was replaced in 1969 by a new station in the same road and in 1994 it was renamed Stratford Police Station.[56] It has been listed as one of the stations to close.

West Ham Police Station, West Ham Lane, Newham, E15 (1969–*c.* 2019).

Woodford Bridge Police Station, Redbridge, London (open *c.* 1913).

Woodford Bridge Police Station

A photograph exists online of a police station at Woodford Bridge dated *c.* 1913 and it is now a veterinary centre.

Woodford Police Station

In 1845 Woodford had two police stations.[57] A new police station was built in 1871 and the address given in 1888 was 'Woodford Wells'.[58] It was closed down when a new station was opened nearby in 1968. Most of the 1871 building was demolished and the site is now residential housing called 'The Mews', but it appears as if parts of the rear of the station have been refurbished into the design of the mews as parts of the cells, and stables have been retained and used in the new development.[59]

The 1968 building is due to close and according to a Freedom of Information request, Woodford Police Station front counter has been closed since 2013, but the police station was still used by the Metropolitan Police for other purposes until recently.

Woodford Police Station, High Road, Woodford Green, Woodford (1968–*c.* 2013).

CHAPTER 6

West London Police Stations

Brentford Police Station

An early Brentford Police Station building still exists at 60 High Street and has the original cells in the basement. It is a Grade II listed building dating from the early eighteenth century and has a nineteenth-century frontage.[1]

Some older residents of Brentford can remember that there was a large three-storey building with a basement in the high street which had been the old Victorian police station. It had opened in 1869 but was demolished in 1969 to make way for the police station and section house designed by J. Innes-Elliot at Half Acre, Brentford. It opened in 1967 and was representative of the 1960s style of architecture. This police station is now closed and there are plans to demolish it and replace it with an arts centre and housing. It was sold in 2015 for £9 million.

A police officer attached to Brentford Police Station was sentenced to four years imprisonment in 1957 for factory breaking and nine charges of shop-breaking, two for stealing property and another twenty-eight offences.[2]

Brentford Police Station, Half Acre, St Paul's Road, Brentford TW8 (1967–2013).

Above: Brentford Police Station, Half Acre, St Paul's Road, Hounslow, TW8 (1967–2013).

Right: Old Brentford Police Station, Brentford 60 High Street, Hounslow (1830–1869).

Chelsea Police Station (Lucan Place)

Chelsea Police Station at Lucan Place was opened in 1939 but was closed in 2013 and sold in 2015 for £40 million. Private developers have submitted plans to develop the site with a ten-storey building. Also under discussion is the use of community space for facilities such as a nursery, post office and doctors' surgeries. It had been preceded by other police stations in the Kings Road, starting with the use of two small houses in the 1830s and the purchase of land from Lord Cadogan in 1850, along with more land and an extensive refurbishment and extension in 1897. The building was not demolished until 1984.

Chelsea Police Station was infamous for the 'Acid Bath' murders, when officers investigated after they became suspicious of the disappearance of a wealthy elderly lady called Mrs Durant-Deacon in 1949. After questioning John Haigh about Mrs Durant-Deacon, as he had reported her missing, he eventually made a statement at Chelsea Police Station that he had 'destroyed her with acid. You will find the sludge that remains at Leopald Road. I did the same with the Hendersons and the McSwans. Every trace has gone. How can you prove murder if there is not a body?' John Haigh was found guilty of murdering Mrs Durant-Deacon and was hanged on the 10 August 1949.[3]

On the 12 July 1959, one of Chelsea Police Station's officers was murdered as he went to apprehend Guenther Podola, who had been a member of Hitler Youth and was wanted for

77

Chelsea Police Station, 2 Lucan Place, Chelsea, SW3 (1939–2013).

burglary and blackmail. He had phoned the person he was blackmailing but his call was traced to a telephone box near South Kensington Underground Station. Detective Sergeant Sandford and Detective Sergeant Raymond Purdy, from Chelsea Police Station, rushed to the telephone box, but during the chase and attempted detention of Podola, Detective Sergeant Purdy was fatally shot.[4] Podola was the last man in Britain to be hanged for murdering a police officer.

Chelsea Police Station (Walton Street)

Walton Street is south of the Brompton road and was seen as a good location for a police station. The rear yard could be accessed from a cul-de-sac at the back of the police station. It is a Grade II listed three-storey yellow brick building, which was built in 1894 and was closed down in 2009. It is still an empty building.

Chelsea Police Station (Walton Street), 60–62 Walton Street, Chelsea, SW3 (1894–2009).

Chiswick Police Station

Records show that there was a police station at Chiswick in 1864, and in 1869 the purchase of land was considered to build a new police station near the 'Windmill' Public House. A purpose-built Victorian building was opened in 1872 in the High Street.[5] It was closed down in 1963 and is now a pub.

A new police station was opened in 1972 on the site of the old fire station. The fire station had been built on the site of Linden House, which had been the home of Thomas Griffiths Wanewright (1794–1847) who was the grandson of the editor of the literary magazine *Monthly Review*. He was an artist and writer but also a fraudster and suspected murderer, with the allegation that he had poisoned members of his family, with one of his victims being a Mrs Abercrombie. The facts are ambiguous as local press reports said that Mrs Abercrombie had been killed with a meat cleaver, rather than poisoned, and indeed Wanewright was pardoned in 1846, dying in Tasmania in 1847. Several books have been written about him.

There were rumours that older members of the fire brigade had heard the footsteps of a woman (assumed to be Mrs Abercrombie) in the basement rooms of the fire station

Above: Chiswick Police Station, 205–211 High Road, Hounslow, (1963–*c.* 2017).

Right: Old Chiswick Police Station, 210 High Road, Chiswick, Hounslow, W4 (1884–1963).

which were originally the cellars of Linden House. The present-day storeroom of Chiswick Police Station is apparently on the same site as the old cellar. It would be interesting to see if there have been any reported sightings or strange noises heard by police officers at the last police station in Chiswick.

Ronnie Biggs, who took part in the Great Train Robbery and spent thirty-six years on the run, was brought back to Britain by private jet and charged at Chiswick Police Station.[6] The station is a leasehold building now closed to the public but police officers from Hammersmith and Fulham are based there while Hammersmith is rebuilt. Hammersmith Police Station is due to reopen in 2020.

Ealing Police Station

A new police station was built at 5 High Street, Ealing, in 1877 and designed by John Butler. The police station was a red brick building with stone dressing with the word 'POLICE' carved in the lintel above the front door. It was demolished in 1972 to make way for a new shopping centre but had been replaced by a new station in 1966 at 67–69 Uxbridge Road. The old Victorian building had been used by the BBC for filming some episodes of *Dixon of Dock Green*, which were shown on television between 1955 and 1976, and the police station featured in the opening titles of the series. The blue lamp used in the *Dixon of Dock Green* series is on display at the Thames River Police Museum.

Ealing Police Station, like many other stations, had seen life in a different division as the result of the reorganisation of boundaries, but by 1966 it was firmly back in 'X' division. 'X' division was created specifically in February 1862 to police the International Exhibition which was held in South Kensington on the site of the present-day Natural History Museum. The division was disbanded after the Exhibition had finished but was reinstated in 1865.[7]

In 1971 Ealing Police Station received new year greetings from the Arab hijacker Leila Khaled. She had been held at Ealing Police Station and had written on the back of airline tickets from the airlines hijacked by the Popular Front for the Liberation of Palestine, which she belonged to.[8] In her later life she was fond of the United Kingdom and corresponded with the two policewomen who were assigned to guard her while she was held at Ealing Police Station.

Old Ealing Police Station, High Street, Ealing, W5 (1877–1966). (Copyright Ealing Archives)

Greenford Police Station,
21 Oldfield Road, Ealing,
UB6 (1896–2018).

Greenford Police Station

The police used a room in a sergeant's house at the police station until he retired when a freehold property was bought from a Mr Bishop for £300. It was adjacent to the White Hart Pub in Oldfield Lane and the purpose-built police station was opened in 1896. It was closed in October 2018 and in May 2019 was still an empty building.

A local newspaper for 1974 has a photograph of an officer at work in the police station garden after he had won an award for gardening.[9]

Harrow Police Station (West Street)

In 1842 a lease was taken out for a police station in West Street, Harrow. The freehold was purchased, and a new police station was built and opened in 1873. By 1936 the Commissioner authorised the acquisition of land for a new police station, as West Street Police station was believed to be very small and inadequate. The new station was eventually opened in 1963 and the old police station was closed down.[10] The West Street building is now used by a school and the 1963 station in Northolt Road is open twenty-four hours a day.

Harrow (West Street) Police
Station, West Street, Harrow
on the Hill, Harrow, HA1
(1873–c. 1963).

Harrow Road Police Station, Harrow Road, Harrow, W9 (1912–2013).

Harrow Road Police Station

An early police station was at 22 Carlton Terrace. Later on, adjacent properties in Woodfield Road were bought. They were situated on a main road and near the toll gate in Harrow Road and close to both the Lock Hospital and the Paddington Workhouse. In 1912 a new police station and section house, designed by John Dixon Butler to a courtyard plan, was opened at 325 Harrow Road. It has been referred to as 'a fine example of a first class town station'.[11] The building has cast iron railings and a lamp standard at the base of the steps with a lantern with blue glass inscribed 'Police' in white and surmounted by a crown.

Harrow Road Police Station, like many other police stations, had a history of being moved from division to division and was designated as a station on 'D' (Marylebone) division in 1859, but transferred to 'X' (Kilburn Divison) in 1864, returning back to 'D' division in 1965 after a revision of police boundaries.

In 1948 a letter was sent to the Commissioner of the Metropolitan Police, Sir Harold Scott, from Jan Read, who worked for J. Arthur Rank, asking for permission and Scotland Yard's assistance to make a film about policing in London called *The Blue Lamp*.[12] The film ended with the death of a police officer, played by Jack Warner, and was actually based on the story of Constable Nat Edgar, who was murdered on duty in 1948. The phrase 'helping police with their enquiries' was first used during the hunt for Edgar's killer.[13] The streets around Harrow Road Police Station were featured in the film *The Blue Lamp* (1950), which was later developed into the TV series *Dixon of Dock Green*.[14]

Harrow Road was the first police station to be filmed behind the scenes for television in a documentary broadcast on BBC1 in 1975. It closed in 2013 and is now luxury private residences.

Northwood Police Station

When the Metropolitan Railway was opened in Northwood near the end of the nineteenth century, the Metropolitan Police were authorised to increase police numbers locally because of the increase in Northwood's population. Although the local freehold owners of land and property objected to the building of a police station and wanted it built in the poorer part of town, it still went ahead and was opened in 1909.[15] Northwood residents

Northwood
Police Station,
2 Murray Road,
Northwood,
Hillingdon, HA6
(1911–2019).

carried on objecting to the police presence. Two cases reached the Kings Bench Division of the High Court for claims of damages, which were settled in favour of the plaintiffs.[16] The early objections of the Northwood residents resulted in a less obtrusive white POLICE lamp being displayed outside the station.[17]

Like many other police stations there have been claims that there is a ghost in the building as a police sergeant committed suicide in one of the cells and has apparently been heard walking from the cells to the station office.[18]

In 1948 a flight from Amsterdam to RAF Northolt collided with an RAF plane over Northwood and thirty-nine people were killed. The accident would have involved assistance from the local emergency services at Northwood.

The station was designed by John Dixon Butler in an Old English style to fit into the semi-rural location. It is a Grade II listed building as it is of special architectural interest as a notable police station by Butler.[19] Pevsner describes it as 'a prominent corner building with deliberately domestic half-timbered frontages in keeping with its' suburban neighbours'.[20] The building opened in 1911 and it has been well preserved with interior features such as the front doors, front desk, staircase, police lamp and 1930s police call box.

Ironically, in spite of the early objections to the building of the police station from local residents, it has been local volunteers who have manned the front desk until it closed down in February 2019. In its place there have been sessions held to speak to the local police at the local Waitrose, Costa, and in a gazebo during good weather.

Norwood Green Police Station

A Metropolitan report of 1864 stated that there was an existing police station in place in Norwood. It was replaced in 1890 by a purpose-built station after the purchase of a piece of land for £215. Norwood Green Police Station policed the local airport at Heston. It was reported that a police officer on early turn duty accepted an offer from a pilot to fly to Jersey while on duty, but came down to earth when he was greeted by a furious senior officer on his return with the words 'Get out of my sight you horrible little man'! He had

Above left and right: Norwood Green Police Station, Norwood Road, Norwood Green, Ealing, (1890–2008).

only been absent from his assigned beat for a short period but had travelled a long distance when he was meant to be policing Norwood! Although he was on tenterhooks for several weeks no further action was taken.[21] The police station is now closed.

Pinner Police Station

Because of the opening of the Metropolitan Railway at Pinner and the subsequent increase in Pinner's population, a police station was opened there in 1892. It was designed by John Dixon Butler but was in a very different style from his usual work as it is less formal and reflects his versatility as an architect.[22] It is a Grade II listed building and protection extends to the stable block and to the police lamps. It is yet another police station claiming a resident ghost as police officers have heard the stairs being used, movement around the cells and papers have been moved around.

A Freedom of Information request stated that the station front office was closed in 2013 but it is still open with a front counter run by volunteers, though its future is uncertain.[23]

Pinner Police Station,
Waxwell Lane,
Pinner, Harrow, HA5
(1899–present day).

Sunbury Police Station

A site was bought for £300 in 1880 in Staines Road and the police station opened two years later.[24] Further extensions were carried out after the purchase of the adjacent property in 1921.

In 1932 Sunbury Police Station was scheduled for closure but there was a protest from Sunbury-on-Thames Urban District Council with a deputation sent to Scotland Yard and received by the Deputy Commissioner, the Honourable Trevor Bingham.[25] A further deputation was seen by the Commissioner Air Vice-Marshal Sir Philip Game on 27 July 1937. The local MP Sir Reginald Blaker questioned the Home Secretary in the House of Commons about the policing of the area, but the Home Secretary replied that as far as he was aware the area would be adequately policed.[26]

In spite of the objections, the police station was closed to the public and a Police Box was erected in the front entrance lobby of the station for use by the public. However, the station continued to be used for parade for duty and for office accommodation. The section house and married quarters were altered and were still used by serving officers. The police station reopened in 1966 but closed between 1992 and 1996 and was transferred to Surrey Police in 2000. As I took a photo of the police station a retired police officer spoke to me and told me that he had served there and found it a lovely police station to work in.

Sunbury Police Station, 189 Staines Road, Sunbury, Spellthorne, TW18 (1880–1998).

Notes

Information on the dates of closure of Metropolitan police stations has been taken from a Freedom of Information request. These figures refer to the closure of police station front offices. Sometimes the date provided by the Metropolitan Police is different if the station has remained open longer. For example, according to the FOI West End Police station closed in 2017 but did not actually close until December 2019.

Information on the sold prices of police stations has mainly been taken from a Freedom of Information request.

Chapter 1: Metropolitan Police Stations

1. (Tottenham-summerhillroad.com/annie_chase_tottenham_memorie.html)
2. (www.exploringsouthwark.co.uk)
3. Kennison, P. and Swinden, D. *Behind the Blue Lamp: Policing North and East London* (Essex: Copperhill Press, 2003)
4. (britishlistedbuildings.co.uk/101393152)
5. Ibid.
6. Kennison, P. *Behind.*
7. Ibid. (All information on the early Metropolitan Police Surveyors in this chapter is from Kennison, P. and Swinden, D., *Behind the Blue Lamp: Policing North and East London (Essex: Copperhill Press, 2003)*

Chapter 2: Central London

1. The Times 5 February 1972, The British Library.
2. Fido, Martin and Keith Skinner, *The Official Encyclopedia of Scotland Yard* (London: Virgin Publishing, 1999)
3. Ibid.
4. (https://www.british-history.ac.uk/survey-london/vol36/pp185-192)
5. Fido, *The Official.*
6. (https://historicengland.org.uk/listing/the-list/list-entry/1066393)
7. The Guardian 14 July 2006
8. Ibid.
9. Best, William C.F. *'C' or St James's: A History of policing in the West End of London 1829-1984 to mark the occasion of the 25th annual reunion of retired officers from 'C' district Metropolitan Police* (Surrey: William Best, 1985).

10. (https://thepolicememorialtrust.org/)
11. Ibid.
12. Ibid.
13. Kennison, P., D.Swinden and Moss, A. *Discovering More Behind the Blue Lamp: Policing Central, North and South West London* (Essex: Coppermill Press, 2014).
14. (https://historicengland.org.uk/listing/the-list/list-entry/1357244)
15. Kennison, P. *Discovering.*
16. *Marti Hari* TNA KV/2
17. *Report on the conditions of the Metropolitan Police Stations, 1 June 1881–30 June 1881* TNA MEPO 4/235
18. *Gerald Road Police Station* TNA MEPO 14/32
19. (https://www.britishpathe.com/video/floral-police-station)
20. Emsley, Clive, *Crime and society in England, 1750-1900* (Oxford: Routledge, 2010)
21. Ibid.
22. Ibid.
23. Ibid.
24. Kennison, P. *Discovering.*
25. Ibid.
26. Fido, *The Official.*
27. Ibid.
28. London Police Pensioner, Metropolitan Police Heritage Centre, Gerald Row Police Station file.
29. *Hyde Park Police Station* TNA MEPO 14/33
30. Ibid.
31. Ibid.
32. Ibid.
33. *Marble Arch: occupation of Marble Arch as a police station* TNA HO 45/3748
34. (https://www.metpolicehistory.co.uk officer-47html)
35. *Marylebone Road Police Station* TNA MEPO 14/37
36. Temple, Philip, Thom, Colin and Saint, Andrew, *Survey of London: South East Marylebone* (New Haven: Yale University Press, 2017)
37. Ibid.
38. Ibid.
39. Ibid.
40. Ibid.
41. Ibid.
42. Ibid.
43. Ibid.
44. Ibid.
45. *Marylebone Road Police Station* TNA MEPO 14/37
46. Kennison, P. *Discovering.*
47. *Report on the conditions of the Metropolitan Police Stations, 1 June 1881–30 June 1881* TNA MEPO 4/235
48. *Marylebone Road Police Station* TNA MEPO 14/37
49. *Area of the Metropolitan Police District* MEPO 2/ 2733
50. Temple, Philip, *Survey of London.*
51. The Evening News 24 February 1970, Metropolitan Police Heritage Centre, Marylebone Police Station file.
52. Daily Mail 10 June 1963, The British Library.
53. Daily Mail 11 November 1897, The British Library.
54. *Report on the conditions of the Metropolitan Police Stations, 1 June 1881–30 June 1881* TNA MEPO 4/235
55. (http://www.nationalarchives.gov.uk/pathways/blackhistory/rights/cato.htm)
56. Fido, Martin, *The Official.*

57. Kennison, P. *Discovering.*
58. Ibid.
59. *Rochester Row Police Station* TNA MEPO 14/37
60. Ibid.
61. (https://historicengland.org.uk/listing/the-list/list-entry/1271080)
62. *Rochester Row Police Station* TNA MEPO 14/37
63. Ibid.
64. *Tottenham Court Road Police Station* TNA MEPO 14/42
65. Ibid.
66. Ibid.
67. Best, William C.F. *'C' or St James's.*
68. The daughter and granddaughter of George Bramwell Vint (1913-1983).
69. Best, William C.F. *'C' or St James's.*
70. Ibid.
71. *Report on the conditions of the Metropolitan Police Stations, 1 June 1881–30 June 1881* TNA MEPO 4/235
72. *Vine Street Police Station* TNA MEPO 14/43
73. *Wellington Arch* TNA HO 45/1890
74. *Report on the conditions of the Metropolitan Police Stations, 1 June 1881–30 June 1881* TNA MEPO 4/235
75. Kennison, P. *Discovering.*
76. Best, William C.F. *'C' or St James's.*
77. Pevsner, Nikolaus, *London: 1, The Cities of London and Westminster* (Middlesex: Penguin, 1973)
78. Frontlines 'Reporting London Good Nick Guide' November 1991 Metropolitan Police Heritage Centre, West End Police Station file.
79. Ibid.

Chapter 3: North London

1. *Albany Street Police Station* TNA MEPO 14/26
2. Ibid.
3. Ibid.
4. Ibid.
5. *Barnet Police Station* TNA MEPO 14/27
6. *Caledonian Road Police Station* TNA MEPO 14/28
7. Kennison, Peter and David Swinden, *Behind the Blue Lamp: policing North and East London* (Essex: Copperhill Press, 2003)
8. Kennison, Peter, *Behind.*
9. (http://www.capitalpunishmentuk.org/rmarwood.html)
10. *Edmonton Police Station* TNA MEPO 14/30
11. (https://historicengland.org.uk/listing/the-list/list-entry/1356643)
12. Kennison, Peter, *Behind.*
13. Wade, Christopher, *The Streets of Hampstead* (London: Camden Historical Society, 2000)
14. *Hampstead Police Station* TNA MEPO 14/33
15. (https://historicengland.org.uk/listing/the-list/list-entry/1130397)
16. Frontlines 'Reporting London Good Nick Guide' November 1991 Metropolitan Police Heritage Centre, Hampstead Police Station file.
17. Ibid.
18. *Highgate Police Station* TNA MEPO 14/33
19. (https://historicengland.org.uk/listing/the-list/list-entry/1379046)
20. *Highgate Police Station* TNA MEPO 14/33
21. Kennison, Peter, *Behind.*
22. Ibid.

23. (https://www.british-history.ac.uk/vch/middx/vol6/pp168-172)
24. *Hornsey Police Station* TNA MEPO 14/33
25. Ibid.
26. (http://www.british-history.ac.uk/vch/middx/vol8/pp82-88)
27. Metropolitan Police Heritage Centre, Islington/Kings Cross Police Station file.
28. (https://historicengland.org.uk/listing/the-list/list-entry/1379124)
29. *Kilburn Police Station* TNA MEPO 14/35
30. Ibid.
31. Ibid.
32. Kennison, Peter, *Behind.*
33. Metropolitan Police Heritage Centre, Kings Cross Police Station file.
34. (https://historicengland.org.uk/listing/the-list/list-entry/1195651)
35. (https://historicengland.org.uk/listing/the-list/list-entry/1207691)
36. (https://www.british-history.ac.uk/survey-london/vol47/pp298-321#h3-0015)
37. *Muswell Hill Police Station* TNA MEPO 14/37
38. Ibid.
39. Elliott, Bryn, *Walthamstow Police Stations 1840-2000* (Waltham Abbey Historical Collection) (http://www.brynelliott.co.uk/index_htm_files/Walthamstow%20Police%20Station.pdf)
40. *Muswell Hill Police Station* TNA MEPO 14/37
41. Ibid.
42. Ibid.
43. (https://www.acornpropertygroup.org/development/station-house-muswell-hill/)
44. Daily Mail 14 February 2015
45. *New Southgate Police Station* TNA MEPO 14/38
46. *St John's Wood Police Station* TNA MEPO 14/41
47. Ibid.
48. *Tottenham Police Station* TNA MEPO 14/44
49. The Evening Standard 31 March 1995, Metropolitan Police Heritage Centre, Tottenham Police Station file.
50. *St Ann's Road Police Station* TNA MEPO 14/41
51. Kennison, Peter, *Behind.*
52. Ibid.
53. *Report on the conditions of the Metropolitan Police Stations, 1 June 1881–30 June 1881* TNA MEPO 4/235
54. *Whetstone Police Station* TNA MEPO 14/44
55. Metropolitan Police Heritage Centre, Whetstone Police Station file.
56. *Willesden Police Station* TNA MEPO 14/44
57. Ibid.
58. (https://www.london.gov.uk/questions/2012/0910)
59. Metropolitan Police Heritage Centre, Willesden Green Police Station file.
60. *Winchmore Hill Police Station* TNA MEPO 14/44
61. (https://www.british-history.ac.uk/vch/middx/vol5/pp142-149)
62. (https://historicengland.org.uk/listing/the-list/list-entry/1189172)
63. (https://governance.enfield.gov.uk/documents/s68067)

Chapter 4: South London

1. (https://jamescousins.com/2013/09/battersea-police-stations-history/)
2. Swinden, David. Kennison, Peter and Moss, Alan, *More Behind the Blue Lamp: policing South and South East London* (Essex: Copperhill Press, 2011
3. Ibid.
4. (https://jamescousins.com/2013/09/battersea-police-stations-history/)
5. Metropolitan Police Heritage Centre, Beckenham Police Station file.

6. Ibid.
7. The Police Review and Parade Gossip 17 June 1896, Metropolitan Police Heritage Centre, Camberwell Police Station file.
8. Ibid.
9. *Camberwell Police Station* TNA MEPO 14/28
10. Ibid.
11. (https://historicengland.org.uk/listing/the-list/list-entry/1378397)
12. Swinden, David, *More.*
13. Ibid.
14. (https://historicengland.org.uk/listing/the-list/list-entry/1080026)
15. Ibid.
16. *Greenwich Police Station* TNA MEPO 14/35
17. (https://historicengland.org.uk/listing/the-list/list-entry/1272459)
18. Fido, *The Official.*
19. *Kingston Police Station* TNA MEPO 14/33
20. Ibid.
21. *Buildings and Fixtures correspondence dealing with the building of a police station at Kingston* TNA MEPO 2/719
22. Ibid.
23. *Kingston Police Station* TNA MEPO 14/33
24. TNA – Kingston
25. *Lee Police Station* TNA MEPO 14/36
26. Ibid.
27. Ibid.
28. Swinden, David, *More.*
29. Ibid.
30. *Lewisham Police Station* TNA MEPO 14/36
31. Swinden, David, *More.*
32. *The Erection of Lewisham Police Station: plans approved* TNA HO 45/9733
33. Swinden, David, *More.*
34. Ibid.
35. *Peckham Police Station* TNA MEPO 14/39
36. Ibid.
37. *Penge Police Station* TNA MEPO 14/39
38. Ibid.
39. *Richmond Police Station* TNA MEPO 14/40
40. Ibid.
41. Swinden, David, *More.*
42. *Southwark Police Station* TNA MEPO 14/41
43. Ibid.
44. *Streatham Police Station* TNA MEPO 14/41
45. Swinden, David, *More.*
46. *Tooting Police Station* TNA MEPO 14/42
47. Ibid.
48. *Occurrence Book Tooting Police Station* TNA MEPO 11/97
49. Evening News 19 August 1976, Metropolitan Police Heritage Centre, Tooting Police Station file.
50. (https://historicengland.org.uk/listing/the-list/list-entry/1385973)
51. Swinden, David, *More.*
52. Daily Mail 18 March 1963.The British Library.
53. (https://historicengland.org.uk/listing/the-list/list-entry/1213983)

Chapter 5: East London

1. *Arbour Square Police Station* TNA MEPO 14/26
2. Ibid.
3. Ibid.
4. Metropolitan Police Heritage Centre, Barking Police Station file.
5. The New Standard 8 February 1981, Metropolitan Police Heritage Centre, Barking Police Station file.
6. Elliott Bryn, *The Stations of J Division: Barkingside* Metropolitan Police Heritage Centre, Barkingside Police Station file.
7. Ibid.
8. Ibid.
9. Kennison, Peter, *Behind*.
10. *Bethnal Green Police Station* TNA MEPO 14/27
11. (http://wilmotst.com/101-bethnal-green-police-station/)
12. The Job Friday 10 November 1995, Metropolitan Police Heritage Centre, Bethnal Green Police Station file.
13. Ibid.
14. *Bethnal Green Police Station* TNA MEPO 14/27
15. The Job Friday 10 November 1995, Metropolitan Police Heritage Centre, Bethnal Green Police Station file.
16. Metropolitan Police Heritage Centre, Bethnal Green Police Station file.
17. (britishlistedbuildings.co.uk/101393152)
18. (http://uniquetoursuk.blogspot.com/2016/02/suffragette-city_16.html)
19. Ibid.
20. Ibid.
21. (britishlistedbuildings.co.uk/101393152)
22. Ibid.
23. (http://wilmotst.com/101-bethnal-green-police-station/)
24. Ibid.
25. *Chadwell Heath Police Station* TNA MEPO 14/28
26. Metropolitan Police Heritage Centre, Chadwell Heath Police Station file.
27. (https://historicengland.org.uk/listing/the-list/list-entry/1065207)
28. Kennison, Peter, *Behind*.
29. *East Ham Police Station* TNA MEPO 14/30
30. https://historicengland.org.uk/listing /the-list/list-entry/1253087
31. *East Ham Police Station* TNA MEPO 14/30
32. Kennison, Peter, *Behind*.
33. *Hackney Police Station* TNA MEPO 14/33
34. Kennison, Peter, *Behind*.
35. Ibid.
36. (https://historicengland.org.uk/listing/the-list/list-entry/1264866)
37. Kennison, Peter, *Behind*.
38. Ibid.
39. The Police Review and Parade Gossip Metropolitan Police Heritage Centre, Hackney Police Station file.
40. *Leman Street Police Station* TNA MEPO 14/36
41. Ibid.
42. Kennison, Peter, *Behind*
43. *North Woolwich Police Station* TNA MEPO 14/38
44. Kennison, Peter, *Behind*

45. Ibid.
46. (www.mola.org.uk/former-old street-magistrates-court-and-police-station-335-and-337-old-street-london-ec1-london)
47. Ibid
48. Metropolitan Police Heritage Centre, Plaistow Police Station file.
49. Elliott Bryn *Walthamstow Police Stations 1840–2000*
50. The Guardian 29 March 2010
51. Metropolitan Police Heritage Centre, Walthamstow Police Station file.
52. Ibid.
53. Elliott Bryn *Walthamstow*
54. Metropolitan Police Heritage Centre, Wanstead Police Station file.
55. Ibid.
56. Kennison, Peter, *Behind.*
57. Elliott Bryn *Woodford Police Stations 1805–2000*
58. *Woodford Police Station* TNA MEPO 14/44
59. Elliott Bryn *Woodford Police Stations 1805–2000*

Chapter 6: West London

1. (https: historicengland.org.uk/listing/the-list/list-entry/1260833)
2. The Times 17 May 1957, The British Library
3. Mass murders committed by John George Haigh at South Kensington and Crawley, Sussex TNA MEPO 3/3128
4. Kennison, P. *Discovering.*
5. *Chiswick Police Station* TNA MEPO 14/28
6. Hammond, Peter and Chiswick Local History Society, *Thomas Griffiths Wanewright* (Chiswick Local History Society Journal number 7 1998)
6. The Independent 7 May 2001
7. *Ealing Police Station* TNA MEPO 14/30
8. Daily Mail Saturday 21 January 1971,The British Library
9. Middlesex County Times 16 August 1974, Ealing Archives.
10. *Harrow Police Station* TNA MEPO 14/33
11. (https://historicengland.org.uk/listing/the-list/list-entry/1263477)
12. Kennison, Peter, *Behind.*
13. Ibid.
14. Ibid.
15. *Northwood Police Station* TNA MEPO 14/38
16. Ibid.
17. Metropolitan Police Heritage Centre, Northwood Police Station file.
18. Ibid.
19. (https://historicengland.org.uk/listing/the-list/list-entry/1392966)
20. Pevsner, Nikolaus, *London: 3, North West* (London: Penguin, 1991)
21. Metropolitan Police Heritage Centre, Norwood Green Police Station file.
22. (https://historicengland.org.uk/listing/the-list/list-entry/1411163)
23. Ibid.
24. *Sunbury Police Station* TNA MEPO 14/44
25. Ibid.
26. Ibid.

Bibliography

Manuscript Sources

The National Archives
TNA MEPO 14/26
TNA MEPO 14/27
TNA MEPO 14/28
TNA MEPO 14/29
TNA MEPO 14/30
TNA MEPO 14/32
TNA MEPO 14/33
TNA MEPO 14/35
TNA MEPO 14/36
TNA MEPO 14/37
TNA MEPO 14/38
TNA MEPO 14/39
TNA MEPO 14/40
TNA MEPO 14/41
TNA MEPO 14/42
TNA MEPO 14/43
TNA MEPO 14/44
TNA MEPO 14/235
TNA MEPO 2/2708

Printed Sources

Secondary sources
Ashley, J., *A Short History of the Metropolitan Police* (London: Metropolitan Police, 1974).
Best, William C. F., '*C' or St James's: History of policing in the West End of London 1829–1984 to mark the occasion of the 25th annual reunion of retired officers from 'C' district Metropolitan Police held at New Scotland Yard on Friday, 8th March 1984* (Surrey: W. C. F. Best, 1985).
Elliott, Bryn, *Woodford Police Stations 1805–2000* (Waltham Abbey Historical Collection) http://www.brynelliott.co.uk/index_htm_files/Woodford%20Police%20Station.pdf
Elliott, Bryn, *Chadwell HeathPolice* http://www.brynelliott.co.uk/index_htm_files/CHADWELL%20HEATH.pdf (Epping Forest District Museum).
Elliott, Bryn, *Walthamstow Police Stations 1840–2000* (Waltham Abbey Historical Collection) http://www.brynelliott.co.uk/index_htm_files/Walthamstow%20Police%20Station.pdf

Emsley, Clive, *Crime and society in England, 1750–1900* (Oxford: Routledge, 2010).

Freedom of Information Request from Metropolitan Police, https://maps.met.police.uk/SysSiteAssets/foi-media/metropolitan-police/disclosure_2017/october_2017/information-rights-unit—a-list-of-police-stations-closed-since-2010-broken-down-by-year).

Kennison, Peter and David Swinden, *Behind the Blue Lamp: Policing North and East London* (Essex: Copperhill Press, 2003).

Kennison, Peter, David Swinden and Alan Moss, *More Behind the Blue Lamp: Policing South and South East London* (Essex: Copperhill Press, 2011).

Kennison, Peter, David Swinden and Alan Moss, *Discovering More Behind the Blue Lamp: Policing Central, North and South West London* (Essex: Copperhill Press, 2014).

Fido, Martin and Keith Skinner, *The Official Encyclopedia of Scotland Yard* (London: Virgin Publishing, 1999).

Pevsner, Nikolaus, *London: 1, The Cities of London and Westminster* (Middlesex: Penguin, 1973).

Pevsner, Nikolaus, *London: 3, North West* (London: Penguin, 1991).

Read, Simon, *Dark City: Crime in wartime London* (Surrey: Ian Allan, 2010).

Temple, Philip, Thom, Colin and Saint, Andrew, *Survey of London: South East Marylebone* (New Haven: Yale University Press, 2017).

Online sources

Police Stations

Barking Police Station: https://www.standard.co.uk/news/london/thirty-people-found-living-in-illegally-converted-east-london-police-station-a2942841.html 8th September 2015.

Battersea Police Station: jamescousins.com/2013/09/Battersea-stations-history

Belgravia Police Station: https://www.london.gov.uk/sites/default/files/pcd_338_part_1_estates_transform_westminster_fbc_feb_2018.pdf

Bethnal Green Police Station: Bethnal Green Police Station includes film footage: http://wilmotst.com/101-bethnal-green-police-station

Bow Police Station: http://uniquetoursuk.blogspot.com/2016/02/suffragette-city_16.html

Bow Street Police Station: 'Bow Street bows out' by James Sturcke: 14 July 2006 - https://www.theguardian.com/uk/2006/jul/14/ukcrime.jamessturcke

Bow Street and Charing Cross Police Stations: https://www.london.gov.uk/sites/default/files/pcd_338_part_1_estates_transform_westminster_fbc_feb_2018.pdf

Brentford Police Station: brentfordhistory.com

Brick Lane Police Office: http://wilmotst.com/101-bethnal-green-police-station

Caledonian Road Police Station: http://www.capital punishmentuk.org/marwood.html

Chelsea Police Station (Lucan Place): http://chelseasociety.org.uk/old-police-station-lucan-place

Chelsea Police Station (Walton Street): 'A steal at £16m: a police station up for sale' https://www.dailymail.co.uk/news/article-1091871/A-steal-16m-police-station-sale.html

Chiswick: Wainewright https://en.wikipedia.org/wiki/Thomas_Griffiths_Wainewright

Chiswick Police Station: https://chiswickherald.co.uk/chiswick-police-station-to-close-p7416-95.htm

Ealing: https: //en.wikipedia.org/wiki/Dixon_of_Dock_Green

East Ham Police Station – 'Mayor 'dismayed' over closure of police station' – 2nd July 2013 - https://www.newham.gov.uk/Pages/News/Mayor-dismayed-over-closure-of-police-station.aspx

Gerald Road Police Station: https://www.londonremembers.com/subjects/gerald-road-police-station

Gerald Road Police Station: https://www.britishpathe.com/video/floral-police-station

Greenwich Police Station: https://www.london.gov.uk/what-we-do/mayors-office-policing-and-crime-mopac/governance-and-decision-making/mopac-decisions–59

Hackney Police Station: http://planningdocs.hackney.gov.uk/Northgathttps://www.hackneycitizen.co.uk/2018/05/04/free-schools-move-hackney-cop-shop-back-on-long-delay/ePublicDocs/00432129.pdf

Hampstead Police Station: https://www.standard.co.uk/news/london/squatters-who-have-taken-over-listed-hampstead-police-station-vow-to-fight-crime-9285964.html

Hampstead Police Station: http://camdennewjournal.com/article/education-chief-old-hampstead-police-station-is-not-suitable-for-new-school

Hampton Police Station: http://www.twickenham-museum.org.uk/detail.php?aid=478&cid=5&ctid=2

Harrow Road Police Station: https://genome.ch.bbc.co.uk/4a66e808dce040059ae665389eabe821

Highbury Vale Police Station: https://www.winkworth.co.uk/properties/11638498/sales/blackstock-road-london-n5/ISL180283

Highbury Vale Police Station: https://www.primelocation.com/new-homes/details/50028005#20AjW0QRr3Zs4TWx.97

Hornsey Police Station: https://www.acornpropertygroup.org/development/station-house-muswell-hill

Muswell Hill Police Station: 24 February 2015 – https://www.dailymail.co.uk/news/article-2953969/This-police-station-looks-like-2015-No-not-break-beat-juice-sipping-PCs-manning-replacements-shut-police-stations-local-Planet-Organic-Costa.html

Northwood: Wikipedia Amsterdam – RAF Air collision 1948.

Northwood: https://www.mynewsmag.co.uk/police-station-will-be-closing-its-doors-for-good

Islington Police Station: https://www.british-history.ac.uk/survey-london/vol8/pp82-88

Leman Street Police Station: 28 October 2013 – https://www.radiotimes.com/news/2013-10-28/the-real-ripper-street-police

Marylebone Police Station: http://www.cushmanwakefield.co.uk/en-gb/news/2018/10/the-portman-estate-completes-the-redevelopment-of-former-marylebone-police-station

Old Street Police Station: - https://www.mola.org.uk/former-old-street-magistrates-court-and-police-station-335-and-337-old-street-london-ec1-london

Old Street Police Station: https://dailymail.co.uk/travel_news/article-3576944

Paddington Green Police Station: Freedom of Information request: https://www.met.police.uk/SysSiteAssets/foi-media/metropolitan-police/disclosure_2017/november_2017/information-right-unit—information-about-paddington-green-police-station

Pinner Police Station: www.harrowtimes.co.uk, Thursday 11 September 2008.

St John's Wood Police Station: https://labourwestminster.wordpress.dom /2014/02/14/8

Tottenham: Tottenham-summerhillroad.com/annie_chase_tottenham_memorie.html

Tottenham Police Station (St Ann's): https://www.haringey.gov.uk/sites/haringeygovuk/files/st_anns_character_appraisal_0.pdf

Tottenham Court Road Police Station: - Friends of the Metropolitan Police Facebook page

Wanstead Police Station: History: 'Iconic Wanstead Police Station sold after 127 years in service' by Rachel Knowles: – 11 November 2013 https://www.guardian-series.co.uk/news/10800473.history-iconic-wanstead-police-station-sold-127-years

Wandsworth Trinity Road Police Station: Wandsworth+Common+Draft+Area+I+Holy+Trinity pdf

Wapping Police Station: https://insidetime.org/the-thames-river-police-4

Willesden Police Station: https://www.london.gov.uk/questions/2012/0910

Wimbledon Police Station: 'High Court hears legal challenge to plans for closures in London' – 8 June 2018 - https://localgovernmentlawyer.co.uk/community-safety/393-community-safety-news/38506-high-court-hears-legal-challenge-to-plans-for-police-station-closures-in-london

Winchmore Hill Police Station: ref: 17/0333141/FUL and 17/03315/LBC - https://governance.enfield.gov.uk/documents/s66021/CAG%20Agenda_31st%20October%202017_Appendix%20D.pdf

www.londonremembers.com/subjects

https://www.metpolicehistory.co.uk women-police.html

http://www.nationalarchives.gov.uk/pathways/blackhistory/rights/cato.htm

Frontlines LPP 'Reporting London Good Nick Guide' 1991 – Metropolitan Police Heritage Centre

General

https://historicengland.org.uk/listing/the-list/list

Mayor of London Office for Policing and Crime: https://www.london.gov.uk/sites/default/files/pcd_338_part_1_estates_transform_westminster_fbc_feb_2018.pdf

'List of Metropolitan Police properties sold' revealed in Freedom of Information requests - 3 September 2018: https://www.standard.co.uk/news/london/revealed-1bn-of-properties-sold-off-by-scotland-yard-a3926436.html

Most London police stations closed to the public two years ago still have not been sold – 3 October 2019: https://www.hackneygazette.co.uk/news/crime-court/most-london-police-stations-closed-to-public-two-years-ago-still-haven-t-been-sold-1-6303751

Plans to close police stations branded 'like a Carry On film' 10 January 2013: https://www.standard.co.uk/news/london/plans-to-close-police-stations-branded-like-a-carry-on-film-8445692.html

Revealed: £1bn of properties sold off by Scotland Yard Monday 3 September 2018: https://www.standard.co.uk/news/london/revealed-1bn-of-properties-sold-off-by-scotland-yard-a3926436.html

Recording of an interview with a retired officer from Marylebone Police Station: https://www.metpolicehistory.co.uk officer-47html

www.exploringsouthwark.co.uk